SHOWCASE OF INTERIOR DESIGN ™

SOUTHERN EDITION

Vitae Publishing, Inc.
Grand Rapids, MI

■

© 1993 Vitae Publishing, Inc.

All rights reserved under International
and Pan-American copyright conventions.
Published in the United States
by Vitae Publishing, Inc.
220 Lyon Street NW
800 Grand Plaza Place
Grand Rapids, MI 49503

■

Library of Congress
Cataloging-in-Publication Data

Showcase of Interior Design, Southern Edition

p.   cm.
Includes indexes.
ISBN 0-9624596-5-8
1. Interior decoration—Southern States—History—20th Century.
I. Newsom, Lisa.
NK2004.S543 1993 729' .0975—dc20 92-31287 CIP

■

VITAE PUBLISHING, INC.

CHAIRMAN—JOHN C. AVES
PRESIDENT—JIM C. MARKLE
DIRECTOR—GREGORY J. DEKKER

■

SOUTHERN EDITION PRODUCTION STAFF

Publishing Director—Sheri L. Rambaud
Communications Coordinator—Cynthia A. Vandecar
Southern Florida Co-Publisher—Gloria Blake, Ph.D.
Greater Dallas Publisher—Arlis Ede
Southeastern Publisher—Betty Ereckson
Associate Publisher—Francine E. Port
Southern Florida Co-Publisher—Susan Preville
Greater Houston Publisher—Sharon Staley
Midwest Publisher—Gita M. Gidwani
Contributing Author—Lisa Newsom, Editor-in-Chief and Publisher of Veranda

■

AVES, INCORPORATED

Art Direction—Carol Dungan
Production Artist—Nancy J. Allen
Production Supervisor—Douglas Koster
Inquiry Management—Jill Nabozny
Financial Management—Robert Spaman

■

Printed in Singapore by Toppan
Typeset in USA by Vitae Publishing, Inc.

■

Title page interior design: Dan Carithers
Photo: Hickey-Robertson

PROLOGUE

■ *Hospitality is a theme that unifies this edition of Showcase of Interior Design. It is a constant aspect of life, from the Southeast to the Southwest. The interior designers who have contributed to this publication all understand the necessity for creating interiors which invite and refresh.*

The value that a professional interior designer adds to the process of creating a satisfying interior is also an important theme, especially for the 90's. More designers are focusing on this aspect of the service they offer. By planning with careful budgets, doing the job right the first time without costly changes and selecting classic design elements that add lasting value to an interior, your interior designer can provide both short and long term investment dividends.

Phone the designers in this edition and ask your questions about budgets and about style. These are people who not only represent their own design practices, but also lead their profession in articulating the role that design can play in creating true value and satisfaction. ■

John C. Aves

TABLE OF CONTENTS

4
■

"SOUTHERN SENSIBILITY" BY LISA NEWSOM

8
■

THE VALUE ADDED BY CAREFUL SELECTION
OF A PROFESSIONAL

14
■

THE A & I PLACE/ANTIQUES & INTERIORS

26
■

AMBIANCE INTERIORS

28
■

CLAUDIA AQUINO INTERIORS

30
■

MARIO ARELLANO INTERIORS, INC.

32
■

GINGER BARBER, INC.

34
■

JOHN BERENSON INTERIOR DESIGN, INC.

36
■

KATRINA BLADES/MICHAEL'S ANTIQUES

38
■

RICHARD BRANCH AND ASSOCIATES

40
■

BRITO INTERIOR DESIGN, INC.

44
■

BROWNS INTERIORS, INC.

46
■

THE BRYAN DESIGN ASSOCIATES

48
■

DAN CARITHERS

50
■

PAULETTE CARRAGHER INTERIORS, INC.

52
■

PATRICIA M. CARSON INTERIOR DESIGN

54
■

LOURDES CATAO & ASSOCIATES, INC.

56
■

CHARLOTTE'S, INC.

58
■

COULSON-HAMLIN

60
■

COVINGTON DESIGN ASSOCIATES, INC.

62
■

JOHN CRAFT INTERIORS

66
■

N. CRAIG INTERIORS

68
■

J. DAYVAULT & ASSOCIATES

70
■

DESIGNERS UNLIMITED, INC.

72
■

PAUL DRAPER & ASSOCIATES

74
■

GILLIAN DRUMMOND INTERIOR DESIGN

76

■

ARLIS EDE, FASID

78

■

STANLEY ELLIS, INC.

80

■

JAMES ESSARY ASSOCIATES, INC.

82

■

WILLIAM R. EUBANKS INTERIOR DESIGN

84

■

AL EVANS INTERIORS, INC.

88

■

FETZER'S INTERIORS & FINE ANTIQUES

90

■

LIZ FISHER INTERIORS

92

■

BILLY W. FRANCIS DESIGN/DECORATION

94

■

GANDY/PEACE, INC.

98

■

LANDY GARDNER INTERIORS

100

■

C. SMITH GRUBBS, INC.

102

■

KATHY GUYTON INTERIORS

104

■

HAIM, FLINT & ASSOCIATES

106

■

KATHERINE HARMAN/THE CORNER CUPBOARD
ANTIQUES AND INTERIORS

108

■

RICHARD HIMMEL

110

■

DAVID HOLCOMB INTERIORS

112

■

RICHARD HOLLEY, INC.

114

■

J/HOWARD DESIGN, INC.

116

■

ROBERT IDOL DESIGN

118

■

INTERIOR DESIGN GROUP, INC.

120

■

CHIP JOHNSTON INTERIORS

122

■

L. BENJAMIN JONES

124

■

RUTH GRAY JULIAN INTERIORS, INC.

126

■

CAROL KLOTZ INTERIORS/REGALO ANTIQUES

128

■

MARTIN KUCKLY ASSOCIATES, INC.

130

■

KUHL DESIGN ASSOCIATES, INC.

134

■

LA MAISON FLEURIE, C.A.

136

■

SUSAN LAPELLE INTERIORS

138

■

R. WARD LARISCY, INC.

140

■

LEET, INC.

142

■

IRENE LEHMAN INTERIORS

144

■

JEANNE LEONARD INTERIORS

146

■

T. GORDON LITTLE INTERIORS

148

■

TON LUYK DESIGNS, INC.

150

■

JUDY R. MALE, ASID, INC.

152

■

MARIE MANSOUR

154

■

ALLAN DAVID MARCUS ASSOCIATES, INC.

156

■

JANE J. MARSDEN ANTIQUES & INTERIORS, INC.

158

■

CLIFFORD STILES McALPIN INTERIORS, INC.

160

■

GENE McINTOSH & ASSOCIATES

162

■

RODGERS MENZIES INTERIOR DESIGN

164

■

M.L. SLOVACK DESIGN, INC.

166

■

MOTZEL-SANS ASSOCIATES

168

■

NICHOLSON INTERIORS

170

■

OETGEN DESIGN AND FINE ANTIQUES, INC.

172

■

JANE PAGE CREATIVE DESIGNS, INC.

174

■

PANKRATZ INTERNATIONAL, INC.

176

■

NANCY PICKARD INTERIORS

178

■

REBECCA

180

■

RILEY-BROWN, INC. INTERIOR DESIGNERS

182

■

SANTI'S INTERIORS, INC.

184

■

SEG INTERIORS, INC.

186

∎

JIMMY SELLARS, INTERIOR DECORATION

188

∎

SCOTT SNYDER, INC.

190

∎

EDWARD H. SPRINGS INTERIORS, INC.

192

∎

SHARON STALEY INTERIORS

194

∎

CARL STEELE ASSOCIATES, INC.

196

∎

JOYCE STOLBERG INTERIORS, INC.

198

∎

STONE-VINING DESIGN ASSOCIATES

200

∎

PAT STOTLER INTERIORS, INC.

202

∎

THRASHER DESIGN COMPANY, INC.

204

∎

SANDI TICKNER INTERIORS

206

∎

DOROTHY H. TRAVIS INTERIORS, INC.

208

∎

RICHARD TRIMBLE & ASSOCIATES, INC.

210

∎

RICKI TUCKER INTERIORS AND CABIN ANTIQUES

212

∎

VANTOSH & ASSOCIATES

214

∎

MICHAEL VON ZURHORST INTERIORS

216

∎

FRANYA WAIDE ANTIQUES & INTERIORS

218

∎

MARIE WARREN INTERIORS

220

∎

J. WESTERFIELD ANTIQUES & INTERIORS, INC.

222

∎

CATHY WHITLOCK, INC.

224

∎

GAIL BRINN WILKINS, INC.

226

∎

YOUNG & COMPANY

228

∎

TOBY ZACK DESIGNS, INC.

230

∎

INDEX OF INTERIOR DESIGNERS

232

∎

INDEX OF PHOTOGRAPHERS

234

∎

SOUTHERN SENSIBILITY

Hospitality is the one word that clearly defines the South. Our welcome mats are freshly swept, our doors always open to friends and guests. We love our homes and we want to share them. Life in the South revolves around a gracious spirit and a deep pride in our heritage, a sense of knowing who we are, where we belong and how abundantly our blessings flow. Above all, we know—indeed, we are taught from the cradle—that to share our bounty with others merely multiplies our appreciation of it.

For many years, our homes, and the way we decorated them, were ignored by national publications, which predominately featured East and West coast residences. While these were often glorious to behold, they did not reflect Southern sensibilities. Then, fifteen years ago, a small group of us produced *Southern Accents.* It struck a resounding chord among readers and soon other regional interior design magazines appeared. *Veranda* magazine, which I founded six years ago as a gallery of Southern style, today enjoys an international readership enchanted by the South's charm and sophistication. Other national publications, eager to participate in the ongoing revelations, now regularly feature Southern homes; indeed, one magazine recently presented three Southern designers in a single issue.

Previously, when decorating a home, trips to New York were a necessity for quality fabrics, furniture and accessories. Now, the South boasts five designer centers and numerous conclaves for antiques and collectibles. In the past, interior designers such as Ruby Ross Wood and Michael Greer, both from Georgia, Billy Baldwin from Maryland and Albert Hadley from Tennessee were forced to practice in New York to

attain universal recognition. Today, our designers are able to stay in the South and still maintain both a national and international following.

Although interior design is a relatively new profession, Southern homeowners have long been interested in their surroundings. After landing at Jamestown in 1607, many settlers augmented their possessions with furnishings made by local craftsmen. As colonists prospered, their homes were adorned with pieces imported from England, France and China. By the mid-eighteenth century, however, Southern artisans were crafting quality furniture, textiles, silver, ironware, pottery and china. That legacy continues to shine—in the colonial lineage of Richmond, Charleston, Baltimore and Savannah, and in the ethnic impact of New Orleans, San Antonio and Miami.

Whether it's a historic plantation framed by trees trailing Spanish moss like Victorian lace handkerchiefs or an eagle's nest of a mountaintop vacation home where the vistas seem to stretch into tomorrow, great design is simply where you find it—and in the South, that's everywhere. Climates, histories and geographies of certain regions have played an important part in the picture.

Florida's semi-tropical landscape and its background as a Spanish colony have stamped indelible marks upon that state's architecture and design. Exteriors and interiors merged into a celebration of the region's glorious sunshine. The generous use of balconies, glazed cloisterways and loggias blended with the Spanish/Moorish concept of patios and terraces as a forerunner to today's popular "Florida room," allowing for gracious but casual entertaining. And, America's preference for lighter colors and simpler forms first originated in this cosmopolitan state. Many Florida designers currently continue to express these popular sentiments in design.

My home state of Georgia, which has become one of the commercial hubs of the New South, presents a wondrously varied design portrait. Hundreds of stately homes bask in their historic Greek Revival architecture, a style popularly identified more than any other with our region of the nation. Traditional decor continues to dominate in the South, and some Georgia designers hark back to early influences, borrowed in part from the Europeans—particularly the English—but fashioned precisely for Southern consumption. Conversely, other area designers don't hesitate before delving into the cutting edge of contemporary images. In between, eclecticism broadens the spectrum so that someone in search of a "different look" never has to gaze for very long before finding it.

Looking westward, the Texas interior design field is as high, wide and handsome—and every bit as remarkably diverse—as the Lone Star State itself. Thus, a Texas designer may drape heavy brocade across the windows of a palatial mansion one day, outfit a West Texas rancher's bunkhouse in suede and khaki the next, and still find time before the month is out to choose twig furniture and chintz for a weekend cabin or rattan chaises and seashell prints for a Gulf Coast beach house. It's all done without the blink of an eye. That's because local designers take a few clues from their neighbors—Deep South traditions on the one hand and Western ruggedness on the other —and refine them with a vital ingredient of their own: daring ingenuity. No matter what the style, period or challenge, Texas designers master the design project with their own brand of bravura.

No matter what state is concerned—be it Alabama, Arkansas, Kentucky, Louisiana, Maryland, Mississippi, Tennessee, Virginia or the Carolinas—Southern homes often bear reminders of the past. Many of the most noteworthy houses in America are found in the South: Stratford Hall, Drayton Hall, Mount Vernon, Monticello, Richardson-Owens-Thomas House and Shadows-on-the-Teche, to name but a few. Most of these national treasures are carefully conserved and open to the public. The region's impressive heritage in the visual arts can be appreciated at the Museum of Early Southern Decorative Arts in Winston- Salem and in Colonial Williamsburg, among several others. All of these places serve to remind us that Southern culture fascinates us all—because the South and culture remain firmly interchangeable.

And what a history it has: a legacy of great prosperity, followed by the nightmare defeat and humiliation in the War Between the States, then after unbelievable hardship, rebirth and new growth. And through it all, the people of the land never lost their manners, their appreciation of fine things and their iron-willed determination.

Some of our ancestors proclaimed that "the South will rise again." Various people have interpreted this phrase with assorted definitions throughout the decades but no one can deny that the dream has indeed come true. As we face the dawn of a new century, the South zooms ahead as the nation's fastest growing region, a thriving complex of industries, businesses and families relocating to our mild climate. The phoenix has once again risen, this time with a Southern accent.

As you look through this book and review with interest the decor of some of the South's finest designers. I think you will realize why Southerners have always believed in themselves. And, why the rest of society is fascinated by our sense of style. After all, it was a Southern woman who, when all seemed lost, fashioned an exquisite dress from the only fabric left—luscious green velvet draperies. Like Scarlett O'Hara, the South and its interior designers have a unique affinity for good taste.

Lisa Newsom

A native of Thomasville, Georgia, Lisa Newsom is the founder, publisher and editor-in-chief of *Veranda* magazine. A co-founder of *Southern Accents* and its former editor-in-chief, she lives in Atlanta with her husband Neal and their four children, Bradley, Leslie, Andrew and Ansley.

OPPOSITE: James Essary Associates, Inc.— Two custom wool needlepoint rugs in taupe and yellow accent an elegant sunroom in Charlotte, North Carolina.

THE VALUE ADDED
BY CAREFUL SELECTION OF A
PROFESSIONAL New York designer Albert Hadley once said, "Above all, I like things that are the reflection of a passionate, cultivated taste, a knowledgeable eye and a stylish gait."

Whether a room is opulent or spartan, traditional or contemporary, each of its features—the furniture, the accents, even the color scheme—tells us about its inhabitant. Walk into the home of a stranger, look around, and you will discover something about that person. The places we live in reflect our dreams, ideas, values and tastes. As we change and grow, our homes evolve. If we can realize how important interiors are to our sense of being, we will recognize the value of interior design and the professional who can help us create satisfying surroundings.

The interior designers on the following pages are experts trained to help us gather our thoughts and stretch our imaginations. They are able to use their experience and knowledge of resources to help us create the best space possible and fulfill our every vision. *Showcase of Interior Design* can help you find a designer who is right for you.

Why hire an interior designer?

Why not? You could go to your nearest furniture or department store and choose a sofa for your new living room. Of course, you will need to arrange a time for its delivery that fits into your schedule. What will you do if that happens to be the same day your painters are scheduled to work? And then, the sofa arrives, and you realize the fabric isn't quite right, and the frame is way out of scale next to your other belongings. Either you pay to have the sofa returned and spend more time searching for another, or you end up with a piece that does not quite fit.

Avoid costly mistakes.

Especially in today's challenging economy, homeowners may avoid interior designers because they fear unmanageable costs. But in reality, designers can help us economize by avoiding costly mistakes. If the sofa seems like a feat in itself, imagine the hundreds of details involved in designing an entire home. With the guidance of a professional, you can eliminate errors, saving time and money. The natural eye, training and experience of designers combine to give them an uncanny ability for envisioning a room before it is finished. Working with scale and color, they are able to orchestrate what was once a cacophony into a symphony.

Every note played on each instrument in a symphony contributes to the success of the concert. The same is true for the success of an interior space, and the professional designer realizes this. No matter how small or seemingly unimportant, each detail of a room is carefully planned in advance. The designer organizes and coordinates every phase of a project so that its final execution is a triumph.

Stretch your budget.

In addition to avoiding costly mistakes, designers further help us economize by stretching our budgets. Designers have an almost unlimited knowledge of resources available in the market. Rather than settling for what is available in the stores, they can help us find the highest quality and most pleasing furniture, wallcoverings, accessories, rugs and carpets for our dollar. Now we can have that "just-right" piece for our home.

Express yourself.

Most of us would like to be fully engaged in the design process. Aside from costs, another major reason many may not use a designer's services is that they fear they will lose their personal identity if they allow an outsider to become involved in the project. It is important to realize that the designer is there, not to impose ideas, but to help clients articulate their own personal style. Think of the designer as an "idea person" who is at your disposal.

Finding the right designer.

Now that we understand the "whys" of an interior designer, we should talk about the "hows." To some of us, the idea of redecorating a small room, much less an entire home, is about as appealing as having a tooth pulled. We would like nothing better than to turn the project over to someone else and hope that the result is to our liking.

Nevertheless, while we appreciate the professional's guidance, most of us would prefer to be involved in every stage of the design process. We hope to find a designer with whom we share a certain chemistry, someone who understands our special needs and is comfortable within our budgetary parameters. This ideal can be achieved with careful research and selection.

OPPOSITE: Richard Branch and Associates — Pale wood walls are a perfect foil for rich fabric and crisp shapes in this eclectic corner.

There is an almost overwhelming field of professionals from which to choose. Begin by talking with friends and colleagues. Find out which designers they have gone to and whether or not they were pleased with the work. The majority of residential designers' work stems from personal referrals and former clients, so this is the best place to start. Also, check with the local chapters of design organizations such as the American Society of Interior Designers (ASID) and the International Society of Interior Designers (ISID). Books, magazines and designer showhouses are also good references, since they provide a visual idea of the designer's work. Just as if you were hiring a new employee, you will still want to check all credentials and references.

What to look for.

Here are some key points to keep in mind as you narrow your choices:

Style. Interview several designers to see actual samples of projects they have completed. Do you like their work? Some designers have a signature style noticeable in all of their rooms. Others focus on the individual taste of their clients. Most designers strive for timelessness in their interiors.

Professionalism. When you check with the designer's past clients, ask whether or not budget requirements were met. Also, does the designer have a history of staying within time frames? Find out whether or not the designer has a support staff to follow up on work.

Compatibility. Since a residential design project is such a personal process, you will want to get along well with your designer from the very start. Do you feel comfortable discussing budgets or voicing your likes and dislikes? Most designers are listeners, but you need to feel as if you are being understood. Pay attention to your own reactions as well as those of the designer.

   Fees. Know the designer's fee structure in advance. Since the relationship will be personal, you want to be straightforward from the beginning. Put everything in writing. A variety of fee structures will be discussed later.

   Come prepared. Do your homework before meeting with the designer for the first time. Be ready to discuss the following:

   Scope of the job. One of the first things the designer will want to know is the size of the project. Are you redoing one room, a suite, an office or an entire home? Will other professionals, such as an architect, be involved?

   Style. Do you follow the Miesian "less is more" philosophy? Or are you more in line with Robert Venturi, believing "less is a bore?" Do you plan to be true to the architecture of the home, or do you prefer a certain period? Organize your thoughts in advance. To create the most satisfying rooms, be as clear as possible about the look you want to create. Bring pictures to help the designer better visualize your ideas.

BELOW: Covington Design Associates, Inc.— Arched windows in a renovated home frame the view of downtown Jacksonville, Florida. The delicate rose motif introduced in the carpeting is echoed in chintz fabrics.

Budget. Be prepared with your budget expectations. The designer will be able to determine if your budget is realistic, whether the project can be completed with the money allocated or if you need to make adjustments.

Money Matters.

Whatever the fee structure you and your designer agree upon, it is important to be up front about costs and payment. Part of the success of your relationship will rely on open communication, particularly in this area. As with any other professional, designers need to feel adequately compensated for their services to perform their best. Most residential designers use some combination of the following:

Design fee/retainer. A design fee is often used to help pay for a designer's creative time and talent. Usually, a deposit or retainer is required before beginning any work. This can be applied to the design fee, or it may be used as insurance of cost coverage should you decide not to proceed with the project.

Mark-up on purchases. For home furnishings, including wallcoverings, furniture, rugs, carpet and decorative accessories, designers become retailers. They buy wholesale and sell retail. The mark-up is called "net plus percentage" in the field. Most of the profit goes toward paying the cost of doing business.

Commissions on labor. For any supervision or coordination of construction or other labor, a percentage of the costs may be charged to cover the designer's time.

Other charges. Renderings, architectural drawings, travel and delivery or shopping in stores that do not offer a designer commission may cost extra. Always ask about special charges.

Consultation fees. Sometimes, you may only need the designer to hang paintings or rearrange furniture. Usually, the designer will charge by the hour or by the day, plus travel expenses.

OPPOSITE: Dorothy H. Travis Interiors, Inc.— Lush greenery encircles an intimate balcony overlooking a spectacular vista.

Designers need to cover insurance and other benefits, fund a retirement plan and pay for a studio or office, along with paying themselves and their assistants. For every dollar designers pay themselves, they spend two for assistance and overhead. This 1-to-2 ratio is common among other professionals as well.

The best relationships are based on open discussions of cost. Review your budget regularly with your designer. This will not only make the process more enjoyable, it will help your designer make prudent selections.

Put it in writing.

To protect both parties, a letter of agreement should be drawn up in advance by the designer, specifying the exact type of services you will receive and under what circumstances they will be performed. New clients are generally asked to send an advance payment.

Beginning the process.

You have chosen a designer with whom you can work with and vice versa. Now, the designer will begin to focus on understanding your likes and dislikes. Do you like blues and greens? Reds and yellows? Do you prefer granite over marble or paint over wallcovering? Do you like flowered chintz or beige linen? You may bring plans or blueprints of the existing space, pictures from magazines or other visual aids to give the designer an idea of your tastes. Some designers take their clients to design centers, others may visit the actual home to get an idea of the client's lifestyle.

Next, the designer creates a scheme with your help. Any architectural or construction work is reviewed. Floor plans are developed based on architectural parameters and an analysis of floor space, traffic patterns, lights, views and the purpose of the rooms. Then, you will begin to make decisions regarding color schemes, fabrics, rugs, window treatments and furniture arrangement.

So that you can visualize the project, the professional puts much research, time and effort into a final presentation. Schemes are presented on boards showing everything from floor plans to specialized surface treatments. You will need to feel at ease with the scheme before approving preliminary budget plans.

Furniture selection is by far the most time-consuming service designers provide. While you will collaborate on this effort, your designer will often pre-shop the market to save time and confusion.

BELOW: Dan Carithers — A timeless bedroom in apricot, soft yellow and green is a retreat into complete luxury.

Dreams materialize.

At the end, the designer turns magician, changing your visions into reality. As the final installation takes place, the designer coordinates work and construction, placing orders and supervising deliveries with apparent ease. Under the designer's harmonizing hand, the last phase provides a dazzling and rewarding culmination.

Using this book.

Showcase of Interior Design is a valuable aid if you are looking for an interior designer. The gifted individuals on the following pages provide you with an impressive pool to choose from. Look through the book, read the philosophies and jot down the names and numbers of a few who spark your interest. Contact them to discuss your project. If you feel compatible, ask for an appointment to review the designer's portfolio and continue your discussion.

OPPOSITE: William R. Eubanks Interior Design — Deep reds and blues accented by royal gold tones envelope a stately study.

THE A&I PLACE/ANTIQUES & INTERIORS

BECKI A. COOK
2021 24TH AVENUE
MERIDIAN, MS 39301
(601) 483-9281   FAX (601) 693-1583

■ *Instinctive use of color, texture and architectural emphasis, elements of contrast and detail which are visually enticing, the combination of the quaint and simple with the distinctive and beautiful, the infusion of the romantic with the whimsical—these are qualities which identify my work. Each client's personality guides me in terms of overall style in an effort to create and capture an elusive charm of timeless, livable interiors.*

All the great periods of decoration in the past were emotional responses to the lifestyle and events of an era. Today, with seemingly unlimited resources and exposure to styles and design, we have the opportunity to choose from the heritage of Old World and contemporary styles in furnishings to express our tastes. Through my interest and involve-ment in antiques and awareness of current developments and concepts, I can perceive an appropriate mix of period decor and selection of quality for my client.

Collaborating with the client, regardless of budget limitations, each design project is a sincere endeavor to fulfill the client's expectations. ■

PROJECTS:
Private Residences: New York City Fifth Avenue apartment; Georgetown condominium; North Carolina beach house; Louisiana historical home; various assignments throughout my area.

CREDENTIALS:
ASID, Allied Member
BS in Art Education
New York School of Interior Design
Parsons School of Design, Paris, France

AMBIANCE INTERIORS

SHARON KISS
2870 PIEDMONT ROAD
ATLANTA, GA 30305
(404) 231-3616   FAX (404) 231-3878

■ *I consider myself most successful when the client is truly excited about the results. One of my primary objectives is to expose clients to goods and resources they would never be able to find on their own. We resource not only from the United States, but from all over the world, including Europe, the Middle East and the Orient. I am comfortable working with traditional or contemporary design, with the objective being to find the best of whatever style makes the client comfortable.* ■

PROJECTS:
Private Residences: In and around Atlanta, Georgia; Beverly Hills and San Francisco, California; New York; and Jacksonville, Florida.

Commercial Work: Atlanta, Georgia.

CREDENTIALS:
New York School of Interior Design
Ohio University
ASID, Associate Member
Atlanta Symphony Decorator
  Showhouses, 1985, 1988, 1989

PUBLISHED IN:
Southern Accents
Southern Homes
Southern Living
HG
Home Magazine's Remodeling
Home Magazine's Kitchen & Bath
Home Magazine's 1001 Home Ideas

CLAUDIA AQUINO INTERIORS

CLAUDIA AQUINO, ISID
3955 NORTHSIDE DRIVE
ATLANTA, GA 30342
(404) 266-9983

■ *My designs
must work for my
clients so that their
homes reflect their
own wants and needs.*

*Just as I can return to
my home filled with all
that I love, my clients
should be able to do
the same. All rooms
should be comfortable
and inviting, yet
elegant. My role is to
skillfully and creative-
ly join beautiful fabric
and furniture with my
clients' personal
touches. I believe that
the testimony of good
design is loving your
home more each day
and never getting tired
of its interiors.* ■

PROJECTS:
Private Residences: Atlanta, Georgia;
Rockland County, New York; Ponte Vedra,
Florida; and Birmingham, Alabama.

Commercial Work: Washington, D.C.;
Atlanta, Georgia; and Georgia State

University Early Childhood Education
Model Day Care Center.

CREDENTIALS:
ISID Georgia Chapter, Board of Directors
Bauder College, Advisory Board
Design for Better Living Award/American
  Wood Council, 1989

Golden Circle Designer of the
  Year/Merchants Association of Miami
Circle Design Center, 1991
Participated in nine Atlanta Design Homes
Vignette for Antique Show benefitting the
  High Museum of Art
Bulloch Hall Antique Showhouse
Southern Living Design Showhouse

PUBLISHED IN:
Southern Living
Southern Accents
Better Homes & Gardens
Creative Ideas for Living
Windows & Walls

MARIO ARELLANO INTERIORS, INC.

MARIO ARELLANO
371 WEST HEATHER DRIVE
KEY BISCAYNE, FL 33149
(305) 361-2744

■ *Most people have strong feelings for their past. So I combine the element of nostalgia with eclecticism to express my client's emotions in their own living space. In order to achieve this result, I must work closely with each client and when finished, I'm pleased when they feel that they are designers too!* ■

PROJECTS:
Private Residences: Mexico; Panama; Colombia; Venezuela; Argentina; New York; Ohio; and Florida.

Commercial Work: England; Bahamas; Puerto Rico; and Havana Hilton and Havana Country Club Restaurant Floridita, Havana, Cuba: Hotel Key Biscayne and Villas, Key Biscayne, Florida.

CREDENTIALS:
ASID

PUBLISHED IN:
Interior Design
Palm Beach Life
Miami Mensual Showcase Property
  Directory

GINGER BARBER, INC.

GINGER BARBER
7026 OLD KATY ROAD, SUITE 164
HOUSTON, TX 77024
(713) 880-2323   FAX (713) 864-5298

■ *I approach each project with careful selection of design elements that complement the existing architecture. An extensive background in both contemporary and traditional interiors is evident in my design work which skillfully combines the classic elements of style, past and present. This is my formula for beautiful interiors, coupled with an intuitive understanding of proportion, texture and color.* ■

PROJECTS:
Private Residences: Houston, Austin, Corpus Christi, Laredo and Rockport, Texas; Los Angeles, California; and London, England.

Commercial Work: Houston, Texas; Los Angeles, California; and London, England.

CREDENTIALS:
ASID
ASID Designer Showcases, 1983, 1985, 1988, 1992
Tiffany's Window Display, 1986
Brevard, Florida Showcase House, 1983

PUBLISHED IN:
Interior Visions by Chris Madden
Houston Metropolitan Remodeling & Decorating, 1992
New York Time, 1989
Houston Home & Garden, 1982, 1984, 1985
Home Magazine, 1984
Houston City Magazine, 1984
Texas Homes, 1983

JOHN BERENSON INTERIOR DESIGN, INC.

JOHN BERENSON, ASID
600 NE 36TH STREET
MIAMI, FL 33137
(305) 573-7007

I approach each design project on an individual basis, since no two clients are alike. I believe good design is that which will have a timeless quality, combining classic periods with just the right element of surprise. A successful space is one that not only appeals to the visual sense, but must also envelop us in comfort. The most successful projects are those where the client and designer are in harmony with one another, allowing the designer to be at his creative best. ■

PROJECTS:
Private Residences: Boston, Massachusetts; Miami, Palm Beach and Naples, Florida; New York; and Virginia.

Commercial Work: Medical Offices and Real Estate Developer's Private Office.

CREDENTIALS:
Boston University, BS, BA
Fashion Institute of Technology School of Interior Design
ASID, Professional Member
IDG "Guilda" Award for Contract Unlimited

PUBLISHED IN:
Florida Designer's Quarterly
Design South
Interior Design

ABOVE LEFT: A melange of classical pieces highlight this sleek deco-inspired dining area at Turnberry Isle.

LEFT: Black granite, pickled wood and glazed lacquer surfaces combine to create an exciting lounge area in this Boston residence.

OPPOSITE: Original French and art deco furnishings provide an opulent backdrop for a Picasso etching in this Boston apartment.

KATRINA BLADES/MICHAEL'S ANTIQUES

KATRINA BLADES
1831 29TH AVENUE SOUTH
BIRMINGHAM, AL 35209
(205) 871-2716

■ *Creating classically designed rooms specifically tailored to each client's individual needs, lifestyle and taste is my primary role as an interior designer.* ■

PROJECTS:
Private Residences: Extensive residential commissions throughout Alabama primarily in the Birmingham area.

Commercial Work: Executive Offices; Doctor Offices; and a Retail Clothing Store.

CREDENTIALS:
University of Alabama, BA
ASID
University of Alabama Outstanding Senior in Interior Design

Alabama Symphony Decorator Showhouses

PUBLISHED IN:
Birmingham Magazine
Birmingham News
Shades Valley Sun News

BELOW: A 19th century Aubusson Portiere used as a bed hanging is the creative element of this bedroom.

OPPOSITE ABOVE: The custom designed needlepoint carpet and the silk taffeta draperies were created for this client's existing furniture in their new Italianate home. All the walls and woodwork are glazed.

OPPOSITE BELOW: These clients wanted a red study. The fabric on the walls is a silk paisley, complemented by a French silk stripe at the windows and a Spanish savonnerie style carpet.

RICHARD BRANCH AND ASSOCIATES

RICHARD BRANCH
2503 ROBINHOOD, SUITE 145
HOUSTON, TX 77005
(713) 524-1424   FAX (713) 524-8291

I believe strongly in the integrity that exists in providing my clients with a sense of ownership in the design process. This is accomplished through mutual respect and a commitment to communicate. With this comes magic! ■

PROJECTS:
Private Residences: Houston and
Simmonton, Texas; Nashville,
Tennessee; New York City; San
Francisco, California; and Singapore.

CREDENTIALS:
Stephen F. Austin State University
University of Houston
ASID, Allied Member
TAID
Winner of 1991 Houston Chronicle/ASID
  Competition

PUBLISHED IN:
Texas Homes
Houston Home and Garden
The Houston Post
The Houston Chronicle

LEFT: The dining room ceiling was mirrored in a compass design to heighten and adorn the lowest ceiling in the house.

OPPOSITE BELOW: The client, an attorney, requested a comfortable residential look for his lobby.

BRITO INTERIOR DESIGN, INC.

ALFREDO BRITO
1000 QUAYSIDE TERRACE, SUITE 412
MIAMI, FL 33138
(305) 895-8539

■ *A great room
is timeless, with
a special appeal that
fulfills all the senses.
The designer creates
an atmosphere by
blending diverse
elements (ie: periods,
styles and colors),
and that atmosphere
is then personalized
by the client's lifestyle
and taste.*■

PROJECTS:
Miami and Tampa, Florida; New York;
Dallas, Texas; Haiti; Mexico; Panama;
Venezuela; Ecuador.

Commercial Work: Corporate offices,
showrooms for modeling and interior furnishings, models, window display.

CREDENTIALS:
MDCC Art Degree
First Place Award Design District, 1988
First Place Award DCOTA Preview, 1990
First Place Award DCOTA Americas
 Conference, 1992
Member of Royal Oak Foundation,
 London, England

PUBLISHED IN:
Design South Magazine
Florida Home and Garden
Gran Libro Decoration
Miami Herald
Vanidades
Selecta
Starlife Magazine
Diario Americas

ABOVE: The passion of red and the
opulence of gold harmonize in this master
bedroom.

RIGHT: This intimate multi-functional
room is enhanced by a mixture of ethnic
accents.

OPPOSITE: The combination of rich materials and styles turned this breakfast area
into a dramatic and elegant dining area.

BROWNS INTERIORS, INC.

E. MORRISON BROWN, ASID
CONSTANCE N. BROWN
1115 KENILWORTH AVENUE
CHARLOTTE, NC 28204
(704) 375-2248

■ *Our residential
and commercial
interior projects begin
with an intellectual
approach based on a
continuing study of
aesthetics and design
appropriateness.*

*A handsome or
beautiful interior
ignores current fads
and trends and
begins with a coordi-
nated architectural
envelope, whether it
exists or has to be
created. It endures
and delights as it
becomes more famil-
iar, comfortably at
home in its setting.* ■

PROJECTS:
Private Residences: North Carolina, South
Carolina and Georgia. Private
Restorations: Albion Plantation in
Winnsboro, South Carolina; The Charles
A. Cannon House in Concord, North
Carolina; and The White Homestead in
Fort Mill, South Carolina.

Commercial Work: Park Meridian Bank;
Banks throughout the Southeast;
Medical, Legal and Executive Offices;
Myers Park Country Club; and Cabarrus
Country Club. Commercial Restorations:
The Grey House (Admissions) and The
Carnegie Guest House at Davidson
College in Davidson, North Carolina.

CREDENTIALS:
E. Morrison Brown, ASID:
Davidson College, Davidson, North
 Carolina, BA
VCU in Richmond, Virginia
ASID
ASID Showhouse Award, Carolinas
 Chapter, 1985
ASID Historic Preservation Award,
 Carolinas Chapter, 1987
ASID Designer of the Year Award,
 Carolinas Chapter, 1987
ASID Honor Award for Design Excellence
 Restoration Design, Carolinas Chapter,
 1992
ASID Honor Award for Design Excellence
 Corporate Design, Carolinas Chapter,
 1992
ASID Honor Award for Design Excellence
 Institutional Design, Carolinas Chapter,
 1992
Board of Directors, Historic Brattonsville,
 South Carolina
Carolinas Chapter Showhouses (26 total)
Peoples Choice Award, Charlotte
Symphony ASID Designer House, 1990

Constance N. Brown:
Washington College, Chestertown,
 Maryland
Texas Woman's University, Denton,
 Texas, BA
University of North Carolina at Chapel
 Hill, North Carolina, MA

PUBLISHED IN:
Southern Accents
Country Decorating Ideas
N.C. Home
The Charlotte Observer
Charlotte Magazine

THE BRYAN DESIGN ASSOCIATES

MARY ANN BRYAN, ASID
PRESIDENT
1502 AUGUSTA #100
HOUSTON, TX 77057
(713) 784-8784

At Bryan Design Associates, we pride ourselves in creating interiors that reflect the unique personalities and needs of our clients.

Designers work separately or together, depending on the size of the project, and are capable of designing in all styles, both residentially and commercially. ■

PROJECTS:
Private Residences: Texas; New York; California; Colorado; and Louisiana.

Commercial Work: Hospitality: Houstonian Hotel, Houston, Texas; Lakeway Inn, Austin, Texas; Marriot at Capitol, Austin, Texas; and Lakewood Yacht Club, Seabrook, Texas. Health Care: Bone and Joint Clinic P.A., Houston, Texas; Village on the Park Retirement Center, Houston, Texas and Villa de Matel, Houston, Texas. Corporate: Anadarko Petroleum Corporation, Houston, Texas; Lockheed Engineering, Houston, Texas and Sterling Consultants, Houston, Texas.

PUBLISHED IN:
Southern Accents
Designers West
Houston Chronicle
Houston Post
First for Women
Houston Home and Garden
Women's World

ABOVE: Spacious dressing area with soaring ceilings offers restful retreat in a botanical setting.

BELOW: Dramatic staircase design enhanced by the addition of the large scaled windows which integrate interior space with a panoramic view.

OPPOSITE: Intimate and inviting living spaces in a grand scaled room.

DAN CARITHERS

DAN CARITHERS
2300 PEACHTREE ROAD NW, SUITE B205
ATLANTA, GA 30309
(404) 355-8661   FAX (404) 355-7480

With each design project, I work closely with my clients to discover what it is that they most like in their interior. We exchange ideas on the mood and essence of the room, colors and their lifestyles. Within all of this, my job is to design an interior that stretches their imagination—a fresh approach to the familiar. In the end, it is most important that my clients find their interiors an extension of themselves, somewhere new and exciting, yet somewhere they call home. ■

PROJECTS:
Private Residences: Atlanta, Georgia; North Carolina; Palm Beach and Hobe Sound, Florida; and Lookout Mountain, Chattanooga, Tennessee. Wedding design consultant for numerous weddings, including Ted Turner's daughters.

CREDENTIALS:
Design Consultant, Baker Furniture
Fashion Merchandise Director, Rich's
 Department Store
Piedmont Ball, Atlanta, Georgia
Guest Speaker at numerous antique shows
 and museums

PUBLISHED IN:
Southern Accents
House Beautiful
HG
Architectural Digest
Veranda

ABOVE: Country dining room with sophisticated charm. Toile at its best and splendid color.

LEFT: Heaviness is stripped away in this living room of classical design with the use of contemporary and fresh colors.

OPPOSITE: Townhouse chic pattern plus color create an enchanting room.

PAULETTE CARRAGHER INTERIORS, INC.

PAULETTE N. CARRAGHER
650 MIAMI CIRCLE NE, SUITE #3
ATLANTA, GA 30324
(404) 261-7981

■ *Decorating is a privilege because not only do I get to express myself creatively, but it also gives me the opportunity to form close and lasting friendships with most of my clients.*

I like traditional rooms with an emphasis on person- ality, rather than historical accuracy. A piece of contemporary furniture or a witty accent can make a room come alive with the personality of the owner.

If I have a signature, it's using yellow and squeezing in a touch of red somewhere. ■

PROJECTS:
Private Residences: Georgia, North Carolina, South Carolina, Florida, New Jersey and New York.

Commercial Work: Nations Bank, Dowden Communications and various Office Projects in the South.

CREDENTIALS:
ISID, Associate Member
Atlanta Symphony Showhouses

PUBLISHED IN:
Atlanta Journal & Constitution
Better Homes & Gardens Decorating
Country Almanac
Creative Loafing
House Beautiful's Top Ten Rooms from
 Showhouse Competition
The Robb Report
Southern Accents
Veranda
Local Publications

PATRICIA M. CARSON INTERIOR DESIGN

PATRICIA M. CARSON
SYKES PLACE PLANTATION
2481 CARSON ROAD
CRAWFORD, MS 39743
(601)328-3033

■ *Investment decorating with the use of antiques is my specialty. I like to create a spirit of informal elegance with a continental mix of furnishings, and am able to create period interiors as well as European contemporary style.*

I work with clients to arrange spaces in which their personal tastes and collections give joy to their lives. Often, the result is an interior which emphasizes warm hues, unique pattern mixes, rich textures and special lighting effects, and most importantly, a timeless undecorated look. ■

PROJECTS:
Private Residences: Mississippi; Alabama; Illinois; Arkansas; and Tennessee. Assistant designer projects in France and Egypt.

Commercial Work: Two model units for a high-rise in Gulf Shores, Alabama.

CREDENTIALS:
Apprenticeship with Bessie Mussey, Inc. (Connoisseur Shop of Birmingham, Alabama)
Leapard's Interiors of Tuscaloosa, Alabama
27 years in interior design

PUBLISHED IN:
New South, 1976
Architectural Digest, 1979
Veranda, 1993

LOURDES CATAO & ASSOCIATES, INC.

MRS. LOURDES CATAO
987 LEXINGTON AVENUE, SUITE 2
NEW YORK, NY 10021
(212) 744-2206

Decorating a home is one of life's most creative endeavors. Therefore, it should not only be a learning experience, but also one that gives great joy.

My design philosophy is quite simple. It is to capture the personalities of my clients in their environment. No two rooms should look alike so that each has an original life of its own. By blending the right combination of colors, textures and light, everything in a room gently becomes part of the total surroundings. Nothing jumps out at you so that each living space reveals itself slowly and discreetly.

Of course, taste and style can be acquired. It is my responsibility to pass that on through my work. Serenity, refinement and the most superior craftsmanship are my only identifiable trademarks. ∎

PROJECTS:
Private Residences: New York City, Oyster Bay, and Long Island, New York; Palm Beach, Brickell Key, and Coral Gables, Florida; New Preston, Connecticut; Paris, France; and Rio de Janeiro, Brazil.

Commercial Work: Delta Bank in Miami, Florida; and Delta Bank, Banco Real, and Banco Economico in New York.

CREDENTIALS:
Institut des Beaux Arts, Paris, France
Royal Oak Foundation Showhouse
Casa Cor, Brazil

PUBLISHED IN:
HG
Home Design
Casa Vogue, Brazil
The New York Times Magazine

CHARLOTTE'S FINE FURNISHINGS

CHARLOTTE KORTH
5411 NORTH MESA
EL PASO, TX 79912
(915)581-1111 FAX (915)581-5478

■ *Decorating is a joyful profession leading to long associations and incredible satisfaction. Our goal is to please our client, and the basic means of reaching this goal is through architecture, scale, color, lighting and carefully placed furniture. We carefully choose accessories, art and antiques, combing the markets and byways for unique treasures. The magic comes when the skillful designer pulls it all together, tending to small details, rearranging here and there...et voila!* ■

PROJECTS:
Private Residences: El Paso, Houston and Dallas, Texas; La Jolla and Palm Springs, California; Arizona; and Mexico.

Commercial Work: El Paso Country Club; Coronado Country Club; Tom Lea Room, University of Texas; Numerous Bank Offices; Stores; and Lawyers' Offices.

CREDENTIALS:
University of Wisconsin
ASID, Professional Member
IBD
Who's Who in Interior Design
University of Texas School of
  Architecture, Advisory Council
El Paso Community College Interior Design Advisory Committee
Committee of 200

PUBLISHED IN:
Architecture Digest
Texas Homes
Ultra Magazine
El Paso Times
El Paso Herald Post

ABOVE: A collage of primitive ancient Santos and Retablos grace the hall chest.

OPPOSITE: The white washed, hand carved wood mantel is a duplicate of Napoleon's carved marble mantel at Fontainebleau.

COULSON-HAMLIN

HARRIET C. COULSON, ASID
ROD L. HAMLIN
2838 BELLEFONTAINE
HOUSTON, TX 77025
(713) 666-1620   FAX (713) 666-3971

■ *We create a unique design which is appropriate for each client's lifestyle and needs— stressing comfort and elegance—but always keeping in mind that good taste is not a function of the budget. Above all, it is important for the client to enjoy the project from beginning to end.* ■

PROJECTS:
Private Residences: Houston, Texas; Santa Fe, New Mexico; Washington, D.C.; and New York City.

CREDENTIALS:
Syracuse University
Parsons School of Design
ASID
First Place Residential ASID Houston
  Chronicle Award, 1990, 1992
Barron's Who's Who in Interior Design
ASID Showhouses, 1983, 1985, 1988,
  1992

PUBLISHED IN:
Houston Post & Chronicle
Designers
Designers West
HG
Houston Home & Garden

COVINGTON DESIGN ASSOCIATES, INC.

CORNELIA COVINGTON SMITHWICK, ASID
3562 ST. JOHNS AVENUE
JACKSONVILLE, FL 32205
(904) 388-0208   FAX (904) 388-9808

'THE COVINGTON COLLECTION'
ANTIQUES, ACCESSORIES, LINENS
3604-2 ST. JOHNS AVENUE
JACKSONVILLE, FL 32205
(904) 388-1668

53 GREEN STREET
LONDON, ENGLAND W1Y 3RH
(071) 499-2364

My work has always reflected the timeless, understated elegance and inviting comfort of the Anglo-American style—a style which provides clients with a traditional, glamorous setting for their treasured collections, yet is eminently suitable for grand or casual entertaining and lifestyles centered around the out of doors, children and pets. ■

COVINGTON DESIGN ASSOCIATES, INC., CONTINUED

PROJECTS:
Private Residences: Florida; New York;
North Carolina; and Maine.

Commercial Work: Executive, Legal and
Medical Offices; Retail Boutiques; and The
Cummer Gallery of Art (Consultant for
1991 Renovation).

CREDENTIALS:
New York School of Interior Design
ASID, Professional Member
ASID Award for Distinguished Service to
  the Society and the Profession, Fall 1990
Appointed by Governor to the first joint
  Florida Board of Architecture and
  Interior Design, 1988
Baron's Who's Who of Interior Design
Florida Interior Design License #1
20 years of experience in interior design
  with extensive world travel and study

PUBLISHED IN:
The Florida Times Union
Florida Real Estate Magazine
Jacksonville Today
Jacksonville Magazine
Town & Country
Veranda, Spring 1991 and 1992, Fall
  1992
Antiques Show Magazine, Wolfson
  Children's Hospital, 1986-91

JOHN CRAFT INTERIORS

JOHN W. CRAFT
3130 MAPLE DRIVE NE, SUITE 1
ATLANTA, GA 30305
(404) 231-4084

■ *Whether the project is traditional or contemporary, large or small, it is most enjoyable when clients allow me to bring about change, to take them where they have not yet been. After a plan is drawn, I love to create mood and atmosphere through color, light, texture and scale; always encouraging clients to "get the background right" before beginning decoration.*

True fulfillment is returning to a project years later to see that it has endured time in quality and beauty. ■

PROJECTS:
Private Residences: Georgia; Alabama; Florida; South Carolina; and California.

Commercial Work: Private Clubs; Banks; Hotels; Restaurants; Auto Dealerships; and Corporate Offices.

CREDENTIALS:
University of Georgia,
  BFA, Interior Design
  Advisory Board
University of Georgia, Interior Design
  Department
House Beautiful Top Ten Showhouse
  Rooms, 1985, 1989
Who's Who in Interior Design
Southeast Designer of the Year Award for
  Residential Work, 1989
Atlanta Decorative Arts Center Award
High Museum of Art Vignettes

PUBLISHED IN:
Interior Visions
Southern Occasions
Fairchild Publications
House Beautiful
House and Garden
Town and Country
Better Homes & Gardens
Interior Design
Veranda
Southern Living
Southern Accents
Southern Homes
Design South
Atlanta Journal & Constitution

N. CRAIG INTERIORS

NANCY CRAIG HOLLINGSWORTH
519 FENTON PLACE
CHARLOTTE, NC 28207
(704) 377-3625

■ *Success as a decorator involves a combination of ability, exposure, sources and organization. I am fortunate to have superior work- rooms and a wonder- fully supportive staff.*

My personal style has been influenced by mentors, Mario Buatta and Jane Williamson, as well as my collecting and extensive travel.

Because I believe our surroundings affect the way we feel, my goal is to interpret the style of my clients and to assist them in incorporating their lifestyle and posses- sions into classic "undecorated" rooms. When I have complet- ed a project, I hope that I leave behind a background in which my clients enjoy comfortable living. ■

PROJECTS:
Private Residences: Charlotte, Lincoln County and Linville, North Carolina; and Charleston and DeBordieu, South Carolina.

Commercial Work: Real Estate, Physician and Corporate Offices.

CREDENTIALS:
Meredith College, BA
Design and Arts Society
Fine Arts Course, Somerley, England

PUBLISHED IN:
Veranda

J. DAYVAULT & ASSOCIATES

JOANNA DAYVAULT JONES, ISID
78 PEACHTREE CIRCLE
ATLANTA, GA 30309-3519
(404) 873-1873   FAX (404) 873-4271

*J. Dayvault &
Associates has a
firm commitment to
communicate and
comply with the needs
of every client, guid-
ing them into educat-
ed selections designed
to produce enduring
comfort, safety and
beauty.* ■

PROJECTS:
Private Residences: Atlanta, Georgia;
Washington, D.C.; New York City;
Birmingham, Alabama; North Carolina;
and South Carolina.

Commercial Work: Noland Company—
Southeastern States; Trust Company Bank
of Atlanta, Georgia; and Medical and
Legal Offices.

CREDENTIALS:
Saint Mary's College
Interior Designer Practice License—
  Washington, D.C.
Georgia Alliance of Interior Design
  Professionals, Member
ISID, Professional Member
ISID, International, First Vice President
ISID, Georgia Chapter, Board Chairman
ISID, Georgia Chapter, President
ISID, Georgia Chapter, Vice President
Who's Who in Interior Design
Atlanta Decorators Showhouse, 6 years
Atlanta Decorators Showhouse,
  Advisory Board Member
Interior design practice since 1965

PUBLISHED IN:
Contract Magazine
Design South
Southern Homes
Atlanta Magazine
Atlanta Journal & Constitution
Accessory Merchandising
Floor Covering Weekly

DESIGNERS UNLIMITED, INC.

CECIL N. HAYES
6601 LYONS ROAD, SUITE C-4
COCONUT CREEK, FL 33073
(305) 570-5843   FAX (305) 570-5862

Cecil's concept of interior design is based on both of her schools of learning — art and interior design. She bases all of her design work on the principles and elements of art. Each space must have a rhythmical flow, balance of objects, a balance of color and texture distribution. Cecil uses space concept and lines of architecture to formulate her first ideas of how a space will accept furniture. Functions and colors are very personal, so in this area she relies upon her clients for their input. ∎

PROJECTS:
Private Residences: Miami, Boca Raton and Palm Beach, Florida; Cape Cod, Maryland; Manhattan, New York; and Birmingham, Alabama.

CREDENTIALS:
Florida A & M University, BS, Art Education
Art Institute of Ft. Lauderdale, Interior Design

PUBLISHED IN:
Magazine of South Florida
Florida Designers Quarterly
Professional Builder
Ideas Magazine
Sun-Sentinel
Shoptalk
Design South
Florida Design
Florida Real Estate

PAUL DRAPER AND ASSOCIATES

PAUL DRAPER
4106 SWISS AVENUE
DALLAS, TX 75204
(214)824-8352   FAX (214)824-0932

■ *The most important element in any design is a rich style that feels as good as it looks. Warmth and comfort can be achieved whether a home is decidedly traditional or contemporary.*
In this way, it can be timeless both in its style and in its inherent ability to evolve.
My greatest reward is a home whose owners could not imagine it any other way. ■

PROJECTS:
Private Residences: Homes throughout the United States and abroad.

Commercial Work: Luxury Hotels, Private Clubs and Restaurants throughout the United States and abroad.

CREDENTIALS:
University of Oregon
Waseda University, Tokyo, Japan

PUBLISHED IN:
Architectural Digest
Interiors
Designers West
Members
Ultra
Travel & Leisure
Restaurants & Hotels International
D Magazine
Detour

COMPENSATION/FEE STRUCTURE:
Varies based on project requirements.

Gillian Drummond Interior Design

GILLIAN DRUMMOND
P.O. BOX 907
GREENWICH, CT 06836
(203) 629-3731

WILMINGTON, NC
(919) 350-0286

■ *My desire is to create a timeless and uniquely personal environment in which my clients can enjoy their lives. A room should, first, serve its* function, and then be comfortable, luxurious and serene, but never take itself too seriously. The combination of color and texture with comfortable upholstery, beautiful woods and unique art and accessories gives a room its personality and style. It should evolve and grow, as we do.
The most important element in the creative process is the mutual trust and communication between designer and client—this is the element that creates the magic. ■

PROJECTS:
Private Residences: North Carolina; South Carolina; New York; New Jersey; Connecticut; Pennsylvania; Maine; and Los Angeles, California.

Commercial Work: Historic Inn and Psychology Counseling Center in North Carolina; Psychiatrist Office in New York; Executive Offices in New York and North Carolina.

CREDENTIALS:
University of Geneva, Switzerland
New York School of Interior Design
B. Altman & Co.
Tate & Hall
Mario Buatta, Inc.
Who's Who in Interior Design, 1991
Who's Who in American Women, 1985-1992
Lower Cape Fear Historical Society Showhouse, 1991
Marketing Consultant to Interior Furnishings Industry

PUBLISHED IN:
North Carolina Homes & Gardens
Wilmington Star News
Wallcoverings Magazine

ABOVE: Entrance gallery in historic renovation for young couple starting an art collection. Dramatic wallpaper framed in doorway at far end adds to the feeling of an art gallery.

ABOVE LEFT: Lush foliage surrounds and is part of this upstairs porch. Black wicker, tropical fabric and hand painted zebra rug on floor give an exotic feel.

BELOW LEFT: Upstairs sitting room is a serene environment to spend quiet time reading, relaxing and listening to music. Regency bench adds to the feeling of "put up your feet and relax." Plantation shutters control the glaring light of a southern exposure.

ARLIS EDE INTERIORS, INC.

ARLIS EDE, FASID
3520 FAIRMOUNT
DALLAS, TX 75219
(214) 521-1302   FAX (214) 521-1355

■ *In Texas, where there are many strong individuals, there is a definite need for a personal design statement that makes the individual feel that his home is distinctly his, with no apologies. Many people need help creating a dream home that is a true reflection of their personal style.*

The personal needs and dreams of my clients are very important to me as a designer. I see my role as the experienced facilitator who works closely with clients, staying within guidelines of budget, space and function, to provide a design solution that is exciting, comfortable and distinctly individual. ■

PROJECTS:
Private Residences: Texas; Florida; and North Carolina.

Commercial Work: Numerous Clubs, Banks and Corporate Offices in Texas and Oklahoma.

CREDENTIALS:
Art Institute of Chicago, BFA
ASID, Fellow
Registered Interior Designer, Texas

BELOW: Living room/dining room of a bachelor's high-rise apartment with a view of downtown Dallas.

OPPOSITE ABOVE: Facilitated client's move from a large home to a high-rise condominium by adapting client's furniture, accessories and antiques to their new home.

OPPOSITE BELOW: A study for a world traveler who collects ethnic art.

Stanley Ellis, Inc.

STANLEY ELLIS
2375 AIRPORT BOULEVARD
MOBILE, AL 36606
(205) 476-8149   FAX (205) 476-8236

145 FIFTEENTH STREET
ATLANTA, GA 30361

■ *My personal objective is creating an interior that reflects my client's personality, taste and needs. I hope that each project is completed in the most creative and successful manner possible.*

I have found my most successful jobs evolve from a close working relationship and exchange of ideas with the client.■

PROJECTS:
Private Residences: New York City; Fredricks, Maryland; Atlanta, Georgia; New Orleans, Louisiana; Washington, D.C.; and Birmingham, Brewton, Tuscaloosa, Mobile, Gulf Shores and Point Clear, Alabama.

Commercial Work: Balsam House Inn in Chestertown, New York; R & R Builders in Fredricks, Maryland; Miller, Hamilton, Snider Law Offices and Coale, Helmsing, Lyons Law Offices, Lewis Advertising, Federal Judge Chambers, Urology Associates, and Surgical Associates in Mobile, Alabama; and The Palms Court in Daytona, Florida.

CREDENTIALS:
University of Delaware
New York School of Design
Robert Simon and Associates, New York

JAMES ESSARY ASSOCIATES, INC.

JAMES WESLEY ESSARY, ASID
P.O. BOX 11857
CHARLOTTE, NC 28220
(704) 552-1796

31 MUSCOGEE AVENUE NW, SUITE 5
ATLANTA, GA 30305
(404) 233-9304

WILLIAM MURPHY, ASID ALLIED

■ As a design team, our hallmark is to achieve a personal style for each client, projecting their individuality and flair, rather than producing a style defined as the designer's work. Understanding and knowing the client well are critical to interpreting their needs and wishes, and translating their dreams into a home of personal comfort, understated beauty, practical livability and lasting pleasure. ■

PROJECTS:
Private Residences: Charlotte, Greensboro, Figure Eight Island and Grandfather Moun-tain Resort, North Carolina; Greenville, Kiawah Island and Litchfield Beach, South Carolina; Atlanta, Savannah, and Skidaway Island, Georgia; Cleveland, Ohio; New York City; and Naples, Florida.

CREDENTIALS:
James Essary:
University of Alabama

ASID Designer of the Year Award, 1988
ASID Residential Honor Award, 1986-91
ASID Showhouse Honor Award, 1986-87
Atlanta Decorators Showhouse
  "People's Choice Award", 1991
Atlanta Decorators Showhouse
  Guest Lecturer, 1992

William Murphy:
East Carolina University Design School
Gardner Webb College, BA
ASID Residential Honor Award
  (Carolinas), 1987-1991

ASID Showhouse Honor Award
  (Charlotte), 1987
Atlanta Decorators Showhouse
  Guest Lecturer, 1992

PUBLISHED IN:
Interior Design Magazine
Southern Accents
North Carolina Homes and Gardens
North Carolina Homes

Southern Living
City Magazine
Peachtree Magazine

ABOVE: English Tudor home displaying plaster parge-work ceiling and red striae walls.

OPPOSITE: Gracious dining room with upholstered walls and draperies of yellow damask.

82

WILLIAM R. EUBANKS INTERIOR DESIGN, INC.

WILLIAM R. EUBANKS
1516 UNION AVENUE
MEMPHIS, TN 38104
(901) 272-1825 FAX (901) 272-1845

■ *Travel has had an enormous influence on my work. The order and timelessness of the Old World hold great appeal for me, and I hope that my work reflects this. Collaborating with clients is a great part of this business. My goal is to create an atmosphere that is personal and exciting and easy to live with at the same time.*

Classic design lends itself to comfort and elegance, wears well over the years and can be added to over time. I feel good design is like great bone structure—the best foundation on which to build. ■

PROJECTS:
Private Residences and Commercial Work:
Memphis, Tennessee and surrounding
areas; Palm Beach, Florida; Kansas City,
Missouri; Houston, Texas; and New York.
Client list available upon request.

PUBLISHED IN:
Southern Accents, 1989, 1991,
  1992
Commercial Appeal (Memphis)
Historic Preservation, 1992

COMPENSATION/FEE STRUCTURE:
Quotations available upon request.

AL EVANS INTERIORS, INC.

AL EVANS
4925 COLLINS AVENUE, SUITE 7A
MIAMI BEACH, FL 33140
(305) 531-5310 FAX (305) 538-0613

■ *One common thread in all my work is that each client gets their own Al Evans! Every component involved in the installation is custom designed in an effort to create humanism and individuality. I interpret my clients' needs to reflect their personalities and guide them with expertise and attention to details.* ■

PROJECTS:
Private Residences: Spain; Central America; Jamaica; England; and in Florida the residences of Roy Black, renowned criminal attorney; Jimmy Cefalo, football celebrity; Dr. Jack Greenberg, heart surgeon; and Lee Schrager, international gala/social coordinator.

Commercial Work: Sandals Hotel Emporium in Jamaica; Alexander Hotel Model Residences in Florida; Corporate Offices of Black & Furci in Florida; and served as set designer for Public Television Channel 17.

CREDENTIALS:
ASID, Signet Award
IDG, Designer of the Year
Awarded by National Boutique Magazine
The Community Alliance Against AIDS,
  Founding Chairman
Florida State License #1467

PUBLISHED IN:
Baron's Who's Who in Interior Design
Design South Magazine, Cover
Palm Beach Life, Cover
The Designer, Cover
Tropic Magazine, The Miami Herald
International television appearances with
  Elizabeth Taylor and Sophia Loren in
  charity projects to benefit the University
  of Miami School of Medicine AIDS programs.

ABOVE: Designer's ocean-front residence.

FETZER'S INTERIORS AND FINE ANTIQUES

NELL G. FETZER, ASID, ISID
711 JEFFERSON HIGHWAY
BATON ROUGE, LA 70806
(504) 927-7420   FAX (504) 927-8280

308 SOUTH HUNTER
ASPEN, CO 81611
(303) 925-5447

534 JACKSON STREET
SAN FRANCISCO, CA 94133
(415) 395-9696

■ *Good design
transcends time!
For over 30 years, I
have assisted three
generations of families
in collecting fine fur-
nishings and design-
ing interiors for their
homes and businesses.
My style is to coordi-
nate with and add to
my clients' collections,
going beyond the art
of decorating. I have
been fortunate to work
with clients who want
to develop and reflect
their good taste.*

*My business has
been built on service.
Tailoring to my
clients' needs satisfies
and makes them feel
comfortable.*

*Upon reflecting on
my many years of
experience, I have dis-
covered the two facets
of my profession that
most please me: mak-
ing spaces beautiful
and making clients
happy.* ■

PROJECTS:
Private Residences: Louisiana; Florida;
Santa Barbara, California; Showcase
Houses in Baton Rouge and New Orleans,
Louisiana and San Francisco, California;
Riverpark Condominiums and the Pearce
Residence in Aspen, Colorado.

Commercial Work: Riverview Medical
Hospital; Guaranty Bank and Trust,
Executive and Branch Offices; Our Lady
of Mercy Church, Activity Center, Baton
Rouge, Louisiana; Gauthier's Restaurant,
Perido Key, Florida; Gourmet Shop,
Atlanta, Georgia; and historical preserva-
tion, specializing in restoration of planta-
tion homes.

CREDENTIALS:
Louisiana State University
ASID, Regional and National Board
 Member
ISID
Louisiana State Licensing Board Member
Anglo American Museum, Board Member

PUBLISHED IN:
HG, 1990
Living With Lace
Garden and Design

ABOVE: English tudor dining room looks
into a warm English living room.

BELOW AND OPPOSITE ABOVE: Old World
17th century Mediterranean style living
room combining all countries and cultures.

OPPOSITE BELOW: Traditional New
Orleans Garden District formal parlor.

LIZ FISHER INTERIORS

LIZ FISHER
1320 SW 15TH STREET
BOCA RATON, FL 33486
(407) 750-4244   FAX (407) 750-1089

CHICAGO, IL
(312) 335-9450

■ *The key to my design approach begins with the client's personality, taste and lifestyle. It is truly a collaboration. What I like is quality and character—quality of things, life, way of living. I look forward to each new project as a creative challenge and welcome the chance to explore new possibilities.* ■

PROJECTS:
Private Residences: Repeat clients from coast to coast. Boca Raton, Palm Beach and Miami, Florida; Lake Forest and Chicago, Illinois; Beverly Hills and Napa, California; and New York City.

Commercial Work: Model Homes; Sales Conference Centers; Executive Offices; Restaurants; and Country Clubs.

CREDENTIALS:
University of Miami
ISID
Florida License #1045

PUBLISHED IN:
Interior Design
Palm Beach Life
Boca Raton Magazine
The Designer
Ideas
Chicago Tribune
Sun Sentinel
Miami Herald
Designers West
Builder Magazine

COMPENSATION/FEE STRUCTURE:
Available upon request.

These photographs are examples of my work, chosen to illustrate the relationship of art to design.

BILLY W. FRANCIS DESIGN/DECORATION

■ *I believe strongly in the importance of these critical design elements—quality, style and appropriateness.* ■

PROJECTS:
Private Residences: Mr. and Mrs. Michael Halbouty and Mr. and Mrs. Charles Hurwitz in Houston, Texas; Dr. and Mrs. Henry Kaufman in New York City; Mr. and Mrs. Stanley Cohen in New York City, Westhampton Beach and Fisher Island, Florida; Mr. and Mrs. Gary Gross in Naples, Florida and London; Dr. and Mrs.

Donald Chambers in Houston and Brenham, Texas and Laguna Beach, California; Mr. and Mrs. Robert Evans in Houston, Texas and Acapulco.

Commercial Work: Greenway Bank & Trust; Boyer, Norton & Blair, Attorneys at Law.

BILLY W. FRANCIS
121 EAST 71ST STREET
NEW YORK, NY 10021
(212) 734-3588

5403 BEVERLY HILL
HOUSTON, TX 77056
(713) 520-6100

CREDENTIALS:
Louisiana Technical University
The New York School of Interior Design
ISID
Member, Interior Design Magazine's
  Hall of Fame, 1988
Baron's Who's Who in Interior Design,
  1990
Architectural Digest—"AD 100," 1990

PUBLISHED IN:
"Decorating Rich"
"Styled for Living"
"International Collection of Interior
  Design"
"Southern Interiors"
Architectural Digest
Interior Design
House Beautiful
Southern Accents
Texas Homes
Homes Magazine
Ultra
Town & Country

GANDY/PEACE, INC.

CHARLES D. GANDY, FASID
WILLIAM B. PEACE
3195 PACES FERRY PLACE NW
ATLANTA, GA 30305
(404) 237-8681   FAX (404) 237-6150

Capturing each individual client's spirit through simplicity, drama and classicism, we emphasize comfort and function in creating interiors that become canvasses for people, artwork and accessories through professional adeptness in lighting, detailing and creativity. ■

PROJECTS:
Private Residences: Atlanta, Georgia;
Cashiers, North Carolina; Ft. Lauderdale
and Naples, Florida; Chicago, Illinois;
Seattle, Washington; San Francisco,
California; Washington, D.C.; Chattanooga
and Knoxville, Tennessee; Tulsa,
Oklahoma; and Antigua, Guatemala.

Commercial Work: Manufacturers'
Showrooms; Restaurants; Hotels; and
Product Design.

CREDENTIALS:
Charles D. Gandy:
Auburn University School of
    Architecture, BID

ASID, Fellow
ASID, National President, 1988

William B. Peace:
University of Kentucky, BA
Recipient of many national and regional
    awards

PUBLISHED IN:
Southern Accents
Interior Design
Southern Living
Southern Homes
Atlanta Magazine
Design South
Designers West
Designers World

LANDY GARDNER INTERIORS

LANDY GARDNER
1903 21ST AVENUE SOUTH
NASHVILLE, TN 37212
(615) 383-1880   FAX (615) 383-4167

■ *Houses must evolve. They must develop over time as an extension of the personality of the family. Each room needs to be a different facet, creating its individual mood as daily routine requires. How a client works, plays, entertains and relaxes is most important when planning interior and exterior spaces.*

Good design is the blending of architecture, lighting, color, pattern texture and comfort. The blending of old and new, of things familiar and things fresh, things proven and things untried. All balanced to be the perfect extension of its inhabitants. ■

C. Smith Grubbs, Inc.

C. SMITH GRUBBS
2054 PALIFOX DRIVE NE
ATLANTA, GA 30307
(404)373-6289

Comfort, livability and the unexpected are Smith's trademarks. Rich layers that appear to have evolved over time reflect the client's life and experiences. Color, texture and a well ordered spontaneity are the result of client and designer collaboration. ■

PROJECTS:
Private Residences: Atlanta, Georgia; New York; Florida; California; and North Carolina.

Commercial Work: Medical Suites, Corporate Offices and Designer Showrooms in Atlanta, Georgia and New York.

CREDENTIALS:
University of North Carolina at Chapel Hill
Randolph College
Southeast Designer of the Year, 1990
House Beautiful's 10 Best Showhouse Rooms, 1989
Best of Show, Langford Elliott Hall, 1989
IFDA

PUBLISHED IN:
House Beautiful
Veranda
Southern Accents
Atlanta Magazine

KATHY GUYTON INTERIORS

KATHY GUYTON
55 BENNETT STREET, SUITE 20
ATLANTA, GA 30309
(404) 352-1113 FAX (404) 352-1130

■ My style is best described as an interesting, easy mix of wonderful things designed for comfortable living. When completed, the home must reflect the taste and interests of the client. The best results are produced when I'm able to incorporate my architectural skills by working closely with the architect and contractor early in a project. My job is to take what is usable, add what is needed, and have the scale, color and texture mix perfectly. In doing this, a timeless, understated elegance is created for a lifetime of enjoyment. ■

RIGHT: Residence in Sea Island, Georgia. Kitchen design, renovation, and decoration by Kathy Guyton.

BELOW: Residence in Washington, D.C.

OPPOSITE: Residence in Atlanta, Georgia.

PROJECTS:
Private Residences: New York City; Hilton Head and Highlands, North Carolina; Atlanta and Sea Island, Georgia; Jackson, Mississippi; Stuart, Florida; and Washington D.C.

Commercial Work: Hotel and Restaurant;

Executive Offices; Doctor's Offices; Private School; Episcopal Church; and Country Club.

CREDENTIALS:
ISID
Best Ten Showhouse Rooms, 1991
22 years of experience in Interior Design

PUBLISHED IN:
Town & Country
House Beautiful
HG
Southern Homes
Metropolitan Homes
Southern Living
Atlanta Homes & Lifestyles

Southern Accents
Veranda
Atlanta Magazine
Atlanta Weekly
Atlanta Journal & Constitution

HAIM, FLINT & ASSOCIATES

FANNY HAIM & BENNY FLINT
21338 W. DIXIE HIGHWAY
N. MIAMI BEACH, FL 33180
(305) 937-0815   FAX (305) 937-3821

■ *Creativity.*
Innovation.
Timelessness. These

elements exemplify our design philosophy. The incorporation of these concepts, along with combined backgrounds in architecture and fine arts, and over twelve years of design experience, has translated into several award winning projects. This unique combination is what ultimately characterizes the firm. This is complemented with strong emphasis on *detail and the use of rich materials and extraordinary art.*

Maintaining client involvement nurtures the design process and assures that the end result is truly a collaboration and therefore, becomes a home. ■

PROJECTS:
Private Residences: South Florida; Colombia, South America; Buenos Aires, Argentina; Jerusalem, Israel; Madrid, Spain; and Caracas, Venezuela.

Commercial Work: South Florida.

CREDENTIALS:
ASID
IDG
Baron's Who's Who in Interior Design
Designer of the Year Award for
   Residential Design Unlimited,
   1986, 1990
Designer of the Year Award for
   Commercial Design Unlimited, 1985
Palm Award for Best Overall
   Residential Design, 1992

PUBLISHED IN:
Florida Designers Quarterly
Vanidades
Design South
Florida Home & Garden
Design World
Southern Accents
New Miami
Miami Herald

BELOW: Award for Overall Best Residential Design, 1992. Lacquered columns flank the arched entry from the living room into the library.

LEFT: Dropped ceilings add architectural detail to this contemporary design.

BELOW: Design of the Year Award for Residential Unlimited, 1990. A collection of fine art became the starting point for this award winning project.

KATHY HARMAN/THE CORNER CUPBOARD ANTIQUES AND INTERIORS

KATHY HARMAN
THE CORNER CUPBOARD ANTIQUES
AND INTERIORS
615 TUXEDO PLACE NW
ATLANTA, GA 30342
(404) 231-9655

■ *To create time-less and uniquely beautiful rooms that are warm and inviting with an understated elegance is my interior design goal.* ■

PROJECTS:
Private Residences: Alabama; Florida; Georgia; Kentucky; North Carolina; West Virginia; and London, England.

Commercial Work: Corporate Headquarters in Atlanta, Georgia; and Executive, Legal and Medical Offices in Georgia and Virginia.

CREDENTIALS:
Queens College
The University of North Carolina
  at Chapel Hill
ISID, Associate Member
Atlanta Decorators Showhouse Participant
Historic Bulloch Hall Showhouse
 "House Beautiful's Ten Best
  Showhouse Rooms", 1986

PUBLISHED IN:
House Beautiful
Southern Accents
Southern Homes
Atlanta Journal & Constitution
Atlanta Homes and Lifestyles
Atlanta Home Restoration and
  Remodeling Guide

RICHARD HIMMEL

PROJECTS:
Commercial Work: Playboy Club and Resort in Lake Geneva, Wisconsin; Marbury Place Hotel in Washington, D.C.; and installations for Victoria's Secret and the Limited clothing store chain. Designed upholstered furniture for Dods-Murdick Transitional Furniture and Baker Furniture Company and Interior Crafts, Incorporated. Country clubs, corporate aircraft, yachts, railroad cars, restaurants, banks and embassies.

CREDENTIALS:
University of Chicago
ASID, Fellow
ASID, former Midwest Chapter President
ASID Designer of Distinction Award, 1992
Interior Design Magazine Hall of Fame
Dean of Dean Design Award, 1987
Euster Award For Outstanding Contributions to the Interior Design Industry, 1982

PUBLISHED IN:
Architectural Digest
Interior Design
Interiors
HG
The Chicago Tribune
The Chicago Sun Times
The New York Times
Numerous other interior design publications

RICHARD HIMMEL
1800 MERCHANDISE MART
CHICAGO, IL 60654
(312) 527-5700   FAX (312) 527-2169

DAVID HOLCOMB INTERIORS

DAVID HOLCOMB
2 VISTA SQUARE NW
ATLANTA, GA 30327
(404) 355-0543

■ We strive to achieve approachable as well as livable interiors that embrace the tastes and requirements of our clients. We always listen to our clients' needs, and then we try to offer new levels of exposure in solving their design needs. Carefully planned solutions are our greatest asset.■

PROJECTS:
Private Residences: Atlanta, Macon, and Sea Island, Georgia; Boston, Massachusetts; Winston-Salem, Charlotte and Roaring Gap, North Carolina; and Spartanburg and Hilton Head, South Carolina.

CREDENTIALS:
The College of William & Mary, BFA
ASID, Former Officer
IFDA
ISID
Decorator Showhouse, Winston-Salem, North Carolina, Junior League
Decorator Showhouse, Charlotte, North Carolina, Symphony
Decorator Showhouse, Atlanta, Georgia, Callenwolde
Decorator Showhouse, Atlanta, Georgia, Alliance Children's Theater

PUBLISHED IN:
HG
House Beautiful
Southern Living
Good Housekeeping
Interiors
Interior Design
Family Circle
Atlanta Journal & Constitution
Charlotte Observer
Winston-Salem Journal & Sentinel

RICHARD HOLLEY, INC.

RICHARD W. HOLLEY
1215 OAKDALE
HOUSTON, TX 77004
(713)524-0066 FAX (713)524-5659

CREDENTIALS:
Pratt Institute, New York
ASID, Allied Member

PUBLISHED IN:
The New York Times Magazine
The New York Times
Interior Views
International Collection of Interior Design
Interior Design
Town & Country
HG
House Beautiful
Houston Home & Garden
Houston Metropolitan
Decorating & Remodeling
Southern Accents
House & Garden, English Edition

J/HOWARD DESIGN, INC.

JUDY HOWARD
25 SEABREEZE AVENUE
DELRAY BEACH, FL 33483
(407) 274-9354   FAX (407) 274-9361

■ *It gives me pleasure to see my clients truly enjoying their homes. This is accomplished by melding my client's individual lifestyle with creativity and attention to detail.*

Ultimately, the most important qualities of each home I design are comfort, beauty, function and the pleasure they bring. ■

PROJECTS:
Private Residences: East Coast of Florida; Chicago, Illinois; Dallas, Texas; and Denver and Vail, Colorado.

Commercial Work: Executive and Medical Offices, Country Clubs, Restaurants, Banks, Model Homes and Yachts.

CREDENTIALS:
University of Colorado, BFA
ASID

ROBERT IDOL DESIGN

ROBERT IDOL
169 AVERY DRIVE NE
ATLANTA, GA 30309
(404) 873-0304

■ *Designers should be great composers, bringing order and beauty to clients' environments. An architectural approach is the hallmark of my work. Clients seek me out for my attention to detail,* *quality of materials, space planning and sense of value.* ■

PROJECTS:
Private Residences: Chicago, Illinois; Los Angeles, San Francisco and Napa Valley, California; Vail, Colorado; Tupelo, Mississippi; and Litchfield, Connecticut.

Commercial Work: Kravet Fabric Showrooms in Atlanta, Georgia; Dallas and Houston, Texas; San Diego and San Francisco, California; Phoenix, Arizona; Dania, Florida; Chicago, Illinois; Philadelphia, Pennsylvania; and Toronto, Canada. Showrooms for Action Industries, a Division of Lane Furniture, in Atlanta, Georgia; Dallas, Texas; High Point, North Carolina; and San Francisco, California. Medical Suites: Dr. Alan Gaynor; Dr. Lee Schwartz; Sunnyvail Convalescent Hospital.

CREDENTIALS:
Randolph College
ASID, Professional Member

PUBLISHED IN:
Designers West
Northern California Homes and Gardens
San Francisco Chronicle
Better Homes & Gardens
The Designer

ABOVE: 1992 Atlanta Showhouse

BELOW: Residence in San Francisco

OPPOSITE: Medical Suite

Interior Design Group, Inc.

EDWARD DAVID NIETO
600 NE 36TH STREET, SUITE 2019
MIAMI, FL 33137
(305) 573-9555   FAX (305) 573-9555

My work reflects the fact that I travel extensively throughout Europe and the Middle East, researching and absorbing the cultural and architectural environments. I interpret the diverse shapes and motifs into each challenge, designing furniture and accessories in traditional or contemporary forms.

This led me to introduce my own furniture line which premiered in the fall of 1992. I feel that each client needs at least some personalized designs in order to express their individuality. ■

PROJECTS:
Private Residences: Spain; France; South America; New York; Washington; Pennsylvania; and Florida.

Commercial Work: Merrill Lynch, Florida; Sivyer Steel Corp., Iowa; and Bloomingdales Showhouse Rooms, 1987-92.

CREDENTIALS:
Philadelphia College of Art
Temple University, BA
ASID
Florida State License #2704
Interior Design Guilds Designer of the
   Year, 1983
Director of Interior Design at
   Bloomingdales, 1987-92

PUBLISHED IN:
Designers West/World Magazine
Design South
The Designer
Florida Home & Garden
Miami Herald
Vanidades
Selecta Magazine

CHIP JOHNSTON INTERIORS

CHIP JOHNSTON
2996 GRANDVIEW AVENUE NE
ATLANTA, GA 30305
(404) 231-4141

CREDENTIALS:
ASID
IFDA

ABOVE: Great Room, Conyers, Georgia.

OPPOSITE ABOVE: Custom Library,
Marietta, Georgia.

OPPOSITE BELOW: Living Room,
Atlanta, Georgia.

L. BENJAMIN JONES

L. BENJAMIN JONES
81 PEACHTREE PLACE #5
ATLANTA, GA 30309
(404) 607-0751

■ *Design should be timeless, comfortable, appropriate and executed with style. Know the rules well enough to break them.* ■

PROJECTS:
Private Residences: Georgia, Florida, Texas, and Oklahoma. Motor yachts: Naples, Florida.

CREDENTIALS:
University of Georgia, BBA

PUBLISHED IN:
Southern Accents
Veranda
Southern Homes
Atlanta Magazine

RUTH GRAY JULIAN INTERIORS, INC.

RUTH GRAY JULIAN, ASID
17331 CLUB HILL DRIVE
DALLAS, TX 75248
(214) 931-3166

■ *I enjoy transforming my client's living spaces into functional, comfortable, beautiful and timeless environments that reflect their individuality. My specialty is making large interiors intimate and elegant and small spaces open and airy. I have the experience and ability to design and decorate in all styles, but enjoy mixing fine reproductions and antiques with contemporary style. I stress quality workmanship and design.*

Confidence is established when the client knows the designer is spending his money wisely, so a budget is always discussed at the time a project is presented. The project should be a fulfilling experience for both the client and designer. My clients become good friends and seek my expertise whenever their lifestyle changes. ■

PROJECTS:
Private Residences: Dallas, Fort Worth and Lake Ray Hubbard, Texas; Washington, D.C.; Chicago, Illinois; New York City; Honolulu, Hawaii; Society Hill Towers, Philadelphia, Pennsylvania; and Stuart, Florida.

Commercial Work: Space Center Memorial Hospital in Houston, Texas; Baylor Medical Center Tower Building, Presbyterian Hospital Professional Buildings One and Two, Woodhill Professional Buildings and Optical Shop in Dallas, Texas; Corporate Apartments on Park Avenue and Fifth Avenue in New York City; and Dallas Symphony Showhouses, 1974 and 1985.

CREDENTIALS:
New York School of Interior Design
Parsons School of Design, Paris, France, French Architecture, Interior Design
ASID, Professional Member
ASID, Board of Directors, Texas Chapter
ASID, Secretary, Texas Chapter
NSID, National Board of Directors
National Trust for Historic Preservation Designer Associate
Washington University, Jewish Hospital School of Nursing, RN
Barnes Hospital–Washington University Medical Center
Post-graduate Studies in Public Health
Cornell–New York Hospital Medical Center
Jersey City Medical Center
Public Health Instructor

PUBLISHED IN:
Dallas Morning News
Dallas Times Herald
Lake Ray Hubbard Magazine
Addison, Texas Register: In Focus

CAROL KLOTZ INTERIORS/REGALO ANTIQUES

CAROL KLOTZ
8 KINGS CIRCLE
ATLANTA, GA 30305
(404)237-4899

■ *My work reflects a love of the Old World charm of Italy and France and the compelling influence of my teacher/mentor, Edith Hills, Atlanta's first Interior Design Hall of Fame member.*

The most evocative word in decorating is "atmosphere"—the spirit, mood and defining element of a room. It is an intangible quality which develops over a period of time as a room takes shape and the tastes and interests of the people who live there become clear. A successful room is comfortable, practical and inviting. It is also original, interesting and well edited.

I like classic rooms,

formal or informal of any period, because they age gracefully and are timeless. Amusing and eclectic additions can keep them current, attention to detail and superior workmanship is what sets them apart. ■

PUBLISHED IN:
Atlanta Journal and Constitution
Southern Homes
Peachtree Magazine
American Design, The South

MARTIN KUCKLY ASSOCIATES, INC.

MARTIN KUCKLY
THAYER DURELL, JR.
506 EAST 74TH STREET
NEW YORK, NY 10021
(212) 772-2228

■ *Our philosophy over the years has always been one of timeless design. We strongly believe that the design should suit both the lifestyle and taste of our clients.*

Our work is always appropriate to the architecture, very personal and generally eclectic with much attention to detail. Working as a team, our office excels at either traditional or contemporary interiors, both residential and commercial. ■

PROJECTS:
Private Residences: New York; Palm Beach, Florida; Jackson Hole, Wyoming; Aspen, Colorado; California; Seal Harbor, Maine; Connecticut; New Jersey; Maryland; North Carolina; New Hampshire; Vermont; Washington, D.C.; Massachusetts; Bermuda; France; and Great Britain.

Commercial Work: The Wauwinet Inn, Nantucket, Massachusetts; Montauk Yacht Club, Montauk, New York; Colony Beach and Tennis Club and Veranda Beach Club, Long Boat Key, Florida; and Numerous Country Clubs and Corporate Offices.

CREDENTIALS:
Parsons School of Design
ASID
National Trust for Historic Preservation, Council Member
Who's Who in Interior Design

KUHL DESIGN ASSOCIATES, INC.

PAMELA KUHL LINSCOMB
KUHL DESIGN ASSOCIATES, INC.
5100 WESTHEIMER, SUITE 200
HOUSTON, TX 77056
(713) 840-1500 FAX (713) 840-1318

CREDENTIALS:
University of Texas, BS
ASID

PUBLISHED IN:
Creative Ideas
Decorating & Remodeling
First for Women
HG
1,001 Home Ideas
House Beautiful
Houston Chronicle
Houston Home & Garden
Houston Metropolitan
The Houston Post
The New York Times Magazine
Southern Accents
Ultra

LA MAISON FLEURIE, C.A.

ANNICK PRESLES
SOPHIE-EVE HOCQUARD
205 WORTH AVENUE
PALM BEACH, FL 33480
(407) 582-9458

CARACAS, VENEZUELA
(582) 752-4909

■ *A dynamic team of two French partners who manage an international firm (Caracas, Palm Beach), focusing on interiors and party decoration. Designing: their passion. Excellence: their goal.*

The designer is like an orchestra conductor who must know how to interpret the client's music and lead a carefully chosen team from the architect to the craftsman. ■

PROJECTS:
Private Residences: Patricia de Cisneros, Venezuela; Maria Luisa De Mendoza, Venezuela; and Mr. and Mrs. Enrico Ghella, Venezuela and Fisher Island, Miami, Florida.

Commercial Work: American Society Ball in Honor of David Rockfeller; Celebration in Honor of Zubin Mehta; Celebration for President Carlos Andres Perez of Venezuela; American Red Cross Showcase House in Palm Beach, Florida, 1991-1992; and Floral Design for Jacqueline de Ribes' Fashion Show, Saks Fifth Avenue, Palm Beach, Florida.

PUBLISHED IN:
HG
Palm Beach Life
Etiqueta

SUSAN LAPELLE INTERIORS

SUSAN B. LAPELLE
500 HUNTERS CROSSING DRIVE
ATLANTA, GA 30328
(404) 671-1272   FAX (404) 671-1272

The process of decorating a space, either residential or commercial, should be as positive as the end result. Timeless rooms are comfortable, practical, pretty and tasteful. The fun comes when there is a whimsical touch and the owner's personality peeks through. This ongoing process works best when it evolves as an honest collaboration between client and designer. As the room is used and the people using the space develop and grow, it should reflect that evolution. With good planning, based on realistic budgets and timing, it can be a most rewarding experience. ■

PROJECTS:
Private Residences: Atlanta, Georgia; Bloomfield Hills, Michigan; Dufuskie Island, North Carolina; Palm Beach, Florida; and Pittsburgh, Pennsylvania.

Commercial Work: Akzo Coatings, Sikkens; Emory University Hospital; Keegan Federal Law Offices; Governor's Pointe; GLG, Inc.; Milner Business Products; Personnel Corporation of America in New York; and Wilen Manufacturing.

CREDENTIALS:
Michigan State University
ISID, Associate Member
Atlanta Decorator Showhouse
Atlanta Historical Society
High Museum Antiques Show

PUBLISHED IN:
Veranda
Peachtree Magazine

ABOVE: Atlanta Decorator Showhouse

BELOW: Executive Office

OPPOSITE: Atlanta Decorator Showhouse

R. WARD LARISCY, INC.

R.WARD LARISCY, ASID
1520 PRUDENTIAL DRIVE
JACKSONVILLE, FL 32207
(904) 396-7886   FAX (904) 396-6499

■ *Function...then beauty...rooms must all function prior to the selection of materials and finishes. Once this has been accomplished, color and pattern take over. I work to bring out the client's personality, and to create an environment that best expresses that personality, whether it is a residential or commercial project.* ■

PROJECTS:
Private Residences: Pittsburgh, Pennsylvania; Washington, D.C.; St. Louis, Missouri; Asheville, North Carolina; Atlanta and Savannah, Georgia; Huntsville, Alabama; Amelia Plantation, Florida — Residence of Chris Evert; and various other residences throughout Florida.

Commercial Work: In Florida: Regency Square Library; Junior League of Jacksonville; Office of Jacksonville Mayor; Jacksonville Eye Center; and Numerous Doctor and Law Offices.

CREDENTIALS:
Auburn University, BA, Interior Design
ASID
Ten Designer Showhouses in Jacksonville
  and Ormond Beach, Florida
Jacksonville Art Museum, Board Member
San Marco Preservation Society,
  Board Member
Florida Community College, Advisory
  Board Member
Florida License #3140

PUBLISHED IN:
Architectural Digest
Southern Accents
Southern Living
Jacksonville Today
Florida Real Estate
"W"

COMPENSATION/FEE:
Retail/Hourly for Design

LEFT: Upholstered walls in Italian silk damask. Antique George III mahogany dining chairs and pedestal table. Silk drapery frame windows overlooking river.

BELOW: A pied-a-terre with every surface hand-painted creating the feel of ancient Pompeii. Antique burnished steel day bed is from France.

OPPOSITE: Wool covered walls surround a faux porphyry fireplace. Antique English painting. Fire screen made from teller's cage.

LEET, INC.

TERENCE S. LEET
812 SEVARD AVENUE
CLEARWATER, FL 34624
(813) 446-5090 FAX (813) 443-7886

■ *I like decorating houses as much as anything I can think of. My philosophy is simple, and I pass it along whenever I can. I keep three things in mind — suitability, which is so important in all aspects, quality and comfort.* ■

PROJECTS:
Private Residences: Clearwater, Sarasota, Tallahassee and Useppa Island, Florida; Vail, Colorado; Harbor Springs, Michigan; and New York City.

CREDENTIALS:
Edinboro College
Parsons School of Design
Parsons, Paris

PUBLISHED IN:
Southern Accents

ABOVE: Leather, linen, against string colored walls. Stark carpet, John Roselli cocktail table. Painting by Dick Jemison.

LEFT: Topiary and trellis design for the courtyard of a house in the Regency Style.

OPPOSITE: Nineteenth century landscape, French club chairs, 1930s floor lamp and antique garden urn against a neutral background.

IRENE LEHMAN INTERIORS

IRENE LEHMAN
7763 SW 102 PLACE
MIAMI, FL 33173
(305) 595-2685 FAX (305) 595-7883

■ *I believe that design should be an enjoyable experience. My clients and I have a truly delightful time together, investing in furniture and accessories that define their taste and lifestyle.*

I feel that people tire of color easily; therefore, I use a monochromatic background of varied natural textures. Color is introduced in art and accessories.

To successfully accomplish each project, I believe it is important to stay within an agreed budget set by the client. ■

PROJECTS:
Private Residences: Miami and Coconut Grove, Florida; Norfolk, Virginia; Deal, New Jersey; East Hills, New York; and Los Angeles, California. Townhomes/ Condominiums: Towers of Quayside in North Miami Beach, L'Hermitage in Coconut Grove, Turnberry Isle in North Miami Beach, The Palace in Miami, Polo Club in Boca Raton and Grove Isle in Coconut Grove, Florida.

CREDENTIALS:
ISID
IDG Designer of the Year

PUBLISHED IN:
Design South
South Florida Home and Garden
Florida Designers Quarterly
Miami Herald
Ideas Magazine

JEANNE LEONARD INTERIORS, INC.

JEANNE LEONARD GOING
1225 U.S. HIGHWAY #1
LOGERHEAD PLAZA
NORTH PALM BEACH, FL 33408
(407) 624-5603

19 MITCHELL ROAD
WESTHAMPTON BEACH, NY 11978
(516) 288-7964

■ *I enjoy the diversity of traditional and contemporary design, whether it be a residential or commercial project. Working closely with my clients to bring out their individual tastes and personalities—creating a warm, comfortable and familiar surrounding to fit the way they live and work is my challenge. My design goal is to have all of my projects remain valid with the passing of time.* ■

PROJECTS:
Private Residences: Manhattan and Long Island, New York; Connecticut; Florida; Vermont; Dorado Beach; Puerto Rico; and St. Thomas.

Commercial Work: Executive Offices of General Electric and Other Major Corporations; Law Firms; Four Long Island Country Clubs; Private Yachts; Restaurants in Long Island and Manhattan; and a Long Island Vineyard.

CREDENTIALS:
New York School of Design
Gold Key Award for Hotel and Restaurant Design
First Place prize in a national contest including prominent hotels and restaurants throughout the United States

PUBLISHED IN:
House Beautiful
House
Woman's Day
Interiors
The New York Times
Newsday
The Daily News
Local Publications

T. Gordon Little Interiors

T. GORDON LITTLE
3133 MAPLE DRIVE, SUITE 115
ATLANTA, GA 30305
(404) 233-0185

■ *In a beautiful room, quite simply, I look for charm, grace, refinement and humor; those lovely qualities almost lost, I am afraid, in a time when excitement, eccentricity and shock are passing for originality and talent. Each day, I see the aesthetic rules being broken one after the other just for effect, apparently even before the rule itself is clearly understood or valued.*

In spite of what the leading "lifestyle" magazines seem to be telling me, I still dream of beautiful rooms sensitively conceived and intelligently executed where lives might be lived with some kind of dignity and calm. ■

LEFT: Private residence in Atlanta, Georgia.

BELOW: Residence of Dr. R. Carter Sutherland and Mr. Holton H. Mastin in Atlanta, Georgia.

OPPOSITE: Residence of Dr. and Mrs. Robert E. Turoff in Atlanta, Georgia.

TON LUYK DESIGNS, INC.

TON LUYK
412 VISCAYA AVENUE
CORAL GABLES, FL 33134
(305) 444-3871 FAX (305) 448-3544

■ *My European background and education have definitely influenced my broad range of design application from classical to contemporary. These elements make a good marriage as the two extremes attract each other; however, high quality is necessary in order for them to complement each other. I like contrast that shocks the silence!*

When designing, one must have the discipline to know when to stop, so the space can grow independently afterwards. ■

PROJECTS:
Private Residences: Miami and Palm Beach, Florida; New York; Boston, Massachusetts; Detroit, Michigan; Seattle, Washington; Palm Springs, California; Nassau, Bahamas; Madrid, Spain; Amsterdam, Holland; Managua, Nicaragua; and Mexico City, Mexico.

Commercial Work: Country Clubs in Palm Beach, Florida; Public Spaces in Palm Beach and Miami, Florida; and Yachts in Greece, Majorca, Spain and Caracas, Venezuela.

CREDENTIALS:
Academy St. Joost in Breda, Holland
Ecole des Arts et Metiers in Vevey, Switzerland

PUBLISHED IN:
Interior Design
Southern Living
Florida Home & Garden
Ideas
The New York Times
Miami New
Miami Herald

JUDI R. MALE ASID, INC.

JUDI MALE
9100 HAMMOCK LAKE DRIVE
MIAMI, FL 33156
(305) 667-8666   FAX (305) 667-2155

■ *The challenge for a designer is learning what makes a client special, and then translating that "specialness" into a unique environment. As the client reveals himself, the designer should be able to communicate that revelation into a functional and beautiful design that flatters and pleases the client. The fun for me, as a designer, is uncovering the many layers of a client's personality, and putting together the various components that provide comfort and satisfaction.*

In my work, I try to steer my clients away from fads and trends, concentrating primarily on architectural integrity, contemporary design, distinctive, quality furniture, and an abundance of the art and "objects" that make environments unique, personal and livable. ■

PROJECTS:
Private Residences: Southern Florida; New York; Los Angeles, California; Aspen, Colorado; and Puerto Rico.

Commercial Work: Corporate and Continuing Care Facilities in Southern Florida, New York, and Boston, Massachusetts.

CREDENTIALS:
University of Miami, BFA, Art History
ASID
Florida State License #155

MARIE MANSOUR

MARIE MANSOUR
7887 SAN FELIPE, SUITE 122
HOUSTON, TX 77063
(713) 781-7601   FAX (713) 988-1940

■ *I believe in not removing myself from my client's own comfort level, but rather merging their taste with my expertise and bringing it a step up from their expectations. Whether it is a work environment, a home or a 170 foot long yacht, it should be livable and a place you love to walk into every day.* ■

PROJECTS:
Private Residences: Large residences in Houston, Dallas and Simonton, Texas; Vail, Snowmass and Aspen, Colorado; and Miami, Florida. One hundred seventy foot yacht originally owned by couturier and perfumer, Coco Chanel.

Commercial Work: Yachts; four large Country and Golf Clubs; Leisure Clubs; Social Clubs; Restaurants; Lounges; Hunting Lodge; and two Banks. More than 500,000 square feet of high-end Commercial Space in Texas; Oklahoma; Denver, Colorado; and New Orleans, Louisiana.

CREDENTIALS:
ASID
Texas Association of Interior Designers
Interior Designer since 1965

PUBLISHED IN:
Designer West, 1980 (cover), 1984, 1986
Boating
Ultra
Houston Home & Garden
Houston Chronicle

COMPENSATION/FEE STRUCTURE:
Depending on intensity of project.

BELOW: Yacht Dining Room

OPPOSITE: Yacht Master Stateroom

ALLEN DAVID MARCUS ASSOCIATES, INC.

ALLEN DAVID MARCUS
4000 TOWERSIDE TERRACE
MIAMI, FL 33138
(305) 892-8920   FAX (305) 899-8929

PROJECTS:
Private Residences: New York City and
West Hampton Beach, New York;
Newport Beach, California; Chicago,
Illinois; Boston, Massachusetts; Palm
Beach, Boca Raton and Williams Island,
Florida; Dallas, Texas; San Juan, Puerto
Rico; and Trinidad.

CREDENTIALS:
Adelphi University
Chicago School of Design
Interior Design Guild
Florida State License #2397

PUBLISHED IN:
Designers West — World Magazine
Design South Magazine
Hotel and Restaurant Design
Palm Beach Life
Florida Designers Quarterly
Palm Beach Post
Miami Beach Magazine
Miami Herald
Florida Design
Florida Homes TV
House in the Hamptons

Good interior design should be classic, traditional and timeless. It should look wonderful today and ten years from today.

I was born into a family who owned a chain of high-end decorating showrooms. That background, coupled with years of technical training and extensive travel, has given me a broad base of understanding and appreciation of all periods of design. I am as comfortable design-ing a traditional pied-a-terre in New York City, as a contemporary California ranch in Newport Beach.

When asked if I have a particular trademark or common theme which is present in all my jobs, I have to smile and admit that I am an avid collector, and I'm guilty of imposing that "curse" on each and every client. "More is more," and even the starkest of interiors has at least one table cluttered with a client's newest collection— be it Limoges boxes, crystal inkwells or English silver frames. ■

JANE J. MARSDEN ANTIQUES & INTERIORS, INC.

JANE J. MARSDEN
JANE MARSDEN WILLIS
2300 PEACHTREE ROAD, #102A
ATLANTA, GA 30309
(404) 355-1288 FAX (404) 355-4552

■ *A good client/ designer relationship is based on the needs of the client. Our goal is to discover what the client's interests and expectations are, and combine their ideas with our professionalism to create a comfortable, livable atmosphere.*

We enjoy working on projects that vary in style, mixing modern and antique, to achieve a diversified look. A room should appear as if it has emerged throughout time, rather than overnight. This philosophy will create a timeless, elegant surrounding suited to the needs of the client. ■

PROJECTS:
Private Residences: Atlanta, Georgia; New York; Washington; and throughout the United States.

Commercial Work: Lanier Plaza Hotel in Atlanta, Georgia; Commercial Buildings and Professional Offices.

CREDENTIALS:
Jane Marsden:
Randolph Macon Women's College
Vanderbilt University

Janie Willis:
Hollins College

PUBLISHED IN:
House Beautiful
Southern Accents
Veranda
Southern Homes
The Architecture of Wm Frank McCall, Jr.,FAIA

CLIFFORD STILES MCALPIN INTERIORS, INC.

CLIFFORD STILES MCALPIN, ASID
900 EAST MORENO STREET
PENSACOLA, FL 32503
(904) 438-8345 FAX (904) 434-8315

■ *The primary goal of decorating should be the appropriateness of the furnishings to the ultimate use of the space. Comfort is also a key element to a successful room, whether it is a bedroom, living room or dining room.*

Quality furniture and accessories are vital to one's long range plan of having a timeless home. Purchases should be made with regard to their ultimate appeal and not for their immediate use.

A comfortable home is a great source of happiness. ■

CREDENTIALS:
University of Alabama, BA
Parsons School of Design, Paris
ASID

GENE MCINTOSH & ASSOCIATES

GENE MCINTOSH, FASID
P.O. BOX 53253
ATLANTA, GA 30355
(404) 352-5712

LAKE OCONEE
(706) 453-2922

■ *Memorable clients, creativity, a sense of good design and appropriateness, restraint, and the ability to interpret and express the client's personality, results in memorable interiors.* ■

PROJECTS:
Private Residences: Georgia and Alabama.

Commercial Work: Corporate Work, Executive Offices and Banks.

CREDENTIALS:
Auburn University, BID
ASID, Fellow
Who's Who in America

RODGERS MENZIES INTERIOR DESIGN

RODGERS MENZIES

KEITH HEADLEY
766 SOUTH WHITE STATION ROAD
MEMPHIS, TN 38117
(901) 761-3161   FAX (901) 763-3993

As interior designers, we feel an obligation to our clients to guide them in achieving a timeless collection of furniture and accessory items. We assist in decisions that will enhance their lifestyle and create surroundings that are rich in detail, yet personal. Most important is an end result that reflects the client's interest and personality, not a predictable, recognizable stamp of the designer. This all must be accomplished without compromising comfort—our byword. ∎

PROJECTS:
Private Residences: Tennessee; Arkansas; Mississippi; Kentucky; Texas; Florida; Alabama; North Carolina; Missouri; and Washington, D.C.

Commercial Work: Medical and Law Offices; Dental Clinics; Private Clubs and Boutiques.

CREDENTIALS:
Rodgers Menzies:
Rhodes College
University of Mississippi

Keith Headley:
Memphis State University
Art Institute of Atlanta

PUBLISHED IN:
Interior Design
Southern Living
Palm Beach Daily News
Memphis Magazine
The Commercial Appeal

ABOVE: Powder room features Chelsea Bird plates.

LEFT: A painting from realist, Mary Sims, enhances a John's Island (Florida) residence.

OPPOSITE, ABOVE: Custom designed floral rug offers foundation for fresh, vibrant color scheme; warms a large room overlooking pool and lake.

OPPOSITE, BELOW: Warm, comfortable setting combines French and English antiques with collections of Meissen, Derby and Imari.

M. L. SLOVACK DESIGN, INC.

MARJORIE SLOVACK
7610 BRYONWOOD
HOUSTON, TX 77055
(713) 956-7240

■ *"What we en-
deavor to achieve
in our surroundings
is an extension of
what we are." To aid
my clients in this dis-
covery is my love
of people and the art
of interior design.
My goal as a designer
is to perceive what
cannot be observed by
those too involved in
their own lives.
Fulfilling needs and
identifying patterns of
living, while applying
classic principles of
design in the manip-
ulation of light, color,
texture and richness of
detail are the hall-
marks of our style.* ■

PROJECTS:
Private Residences: Houston, Austin
and Dallas, Texas; Aspen, Colorado;
Palm Springs, California; Grosse Pointe,
Michigan; Hinsdale, Illinois; New
Hampshire; New Jersey; Chub Cay,
Bahamas; and London's Eaton Square.

Commercial Work: "Krispen's" Antiques
in Galleria II, Houston, Texas; Private
Clubhouses in Texas and Tennessee;
Models; and Office Suites.

CREDENTIALS:
University of Houston, Art
ASID, Allied Member
TAID
ASID Chronicle Award Recipient, 1992
ASID Designer Showhouse, 1992
Texas Interior Design License
Extensive travel and acquisitions of
antiques for client collections

PUBLISHED IN:
Houston Home & Garden
Houston Chronicle
Houston Post
Better Homes & Gardens
Several remodeling magazines

MOTZEL-SANS ASSOCIATES

VINCENT MOTZEL
ARIEL SANS
7200 SOUTH FEDERAL HIGHWAY
HYPOLUXO, FL 33462
(407)547-7550   FAX (407)547-7549

■ *Our firm is dedicated to bringing to our clients fresh new approaches to classical eclectic design. While both contemporary and traditional furnishings and ideas are used, all of our work is planned to become everlasting growing environments for our clients. If we are known for anything, it is that we mirror the personalities of our clients perfectly.* ■

PROJECTS:
Private Residences: New York; Philadelphia, Pennsylvania; Boston, Massachusetts; New Jersey; Washington, D.C.; Miami and Palm Beach, Florida; and Mexico.

CREDENTIALS:
More than 25 years of practical experience designing for hundreds of clients.

PUBLISHED IN:
Philadelphia Enquirer
Miami Herald
Palm Beach Life
South Florida Real Estate
Florida Designers Quarterly
Ft. Lauderdale Sun Sentinel

ALL PHOTOS: The photos shown are of a Florida home designed for a client who is a major collector of contemporary art. Every design element and every piece of furniture was chosen to enhance the extensive collection of art that is displayed throughout the interior and exterior of the house. Artists represented are Calder, Henry Moore, DuBuffet, Appel, Gilbert and George, Natkin and others.

NICHOLSON INTERIORS

LOUIS R. NICHOLSON, ASID
1810 WEST 35TH STREET
AUSTIN, TX 78703
(512) 458-6395 FAX (512) 454-1035

■ *A commitment to style, quality and suitability with respect for our patrons' preferences and lifestyles. After all, there's no place like home.* ■

PROJECTS:
Private Residences: Austin, Dallas, Houston, San Antonio and the Rio Grande Valley of Texas; San Francisco and La Jolla, California; Mexico City, Tampico and San Miguel De Allende, Mexico; and White Sulphur Springs, West Virginia.

Commercial Work: ATT Regional Office Center, Headliners Club, Delta Delta Delta Sorority, Kappa Alpha Theta Sorority and Dr. Robert A. Ersek, Plastic Surgeon in Austin, Texas; and Coca-Cola Company in Tampico, Mexico.

CREDENTIALS:
University of Texas, Austin
ASID, Professional Member for 26 years
Texas Sesquicentennial Showhouse, Dallas
Austin Women's Symphony League, nine annual Showhouses

PUBLISHED IN:
Texas Homes Magazine
HG
Austin Homes and Gardens Magazine
The American Statesman
Successful Attitudes
The Designer Buyers Guide (cover)

ABOVE LEFT: The animals natural coloration dictated the scheme. Though 3200 square feet in size, we were able to make this space livable through scale and lighting design elements. Architecture by Stephen Kubenka, AIA.

BELOW LEFT: 1855 French scenic paper, a fine French chandelier above antique furnishings and red damask walls. Architecture by Stephen Kubenka, AIA.

OPPOSITE: The parlour of historic Sweetbrush Estate, Austin, Texas (1852) in its happiest palette of its 140 years. Lead print fabric—Brunschwig-Fils.

Oetgen Design and Fine Antiques, Inc.

JOHN D. OETGEN
PAIGE S. HENRY
2300 PEACHTREE ROAD NW
ATLANTA, GA 30309
(404) 352-1112

PUBLISHED IN:
"Interior Visions, Great American
   Designers and the Showhouse"
"From Plantation to Peachtree"
HG, 11/91, 4/92
House Beautiful, 5/91
Southern Accents, 3/91
Veranda
Southern Homes
"W"
Atlanta Magazine
Interior Design
Better Homes & Gardens
Restaurant & Hospitality
Atlanta Journal & Constitution
Atlanta Business Chronicle
Peachtree Magazine
Washington Dossier

CREDENTIALS:
Woodruff Memorial Arts Center, Atlanta
Swan Coach House, Atlanta History
   Center
Georgia Trust for Historic Preservation
Atlanta Symphony Decorators
   Showhouse
Egleston Children's Hospital Festival of
   Trees
Atlanta Arts Festival
Tiffany & Co.
Heath Gallery, Atlanta
Nexus Art Center, Atlanta

JANE PAGE CREATIVE DESIGNS, INC.

JANE PAGE CRUMP, ASID
5120 WOODWAY, SUITE 10002
HOUSTON, TX 77056
(713) 871-8053   FAX (713) 439-0148

■ *Timeless, understated elegance is my design goal, whether working with contemporary or traditional design. I approach a job by first assessing the architectural interests of the space; if there are none, I try to integrate architectural elements into my design solution. I feel a professional responsibility to explore several design possibilities before presenting the best two or three for my client's consideration. Working together, we can then develop an overall design based on the client's taste, lifestyle and budget. I do encourage my clients to consider the "basic wardrobe" theory: buy things that you love, and think of them as investments!*■

PROJECTS:
Private Residences: Texas; Oklahoma; and Arizona.

Commercial Work: Corporate Executive Offices at Shell Oil and Price Waterhouse, among others; Medical Offices; Hotel Public Space; and Retail Space.

CREDENTIALS:
University of Texas, MBA
ASID, President, Texas Gulf Coast Chapter
International Illumination Award of Merit, 1986
State Award for Lighting Design (IES), 1986
Display Award, Gift & Accessories Magazine, 1985
Houston ASID Showhouses, 1979, 1981, 1983, 1985, 1986, 1988, 1992

PUBLISHED IN:
Kitchens By Professional Designers, Book IV
Baths & More, Book II
Designer Specifier
Builder/Architect
Houston Chronicle Lifestyle
Houston Post
Kitchen & Bath Concepts
Kitchen & Bath Business
Home Entertainment
Lighting Design & Application

PANKRATZ, INC. DESIGN/DECORATION

TERY PANKRATZ
1115 SOUTHWEST 5TH PLACE
FT. LAUDERDALE, FL 33312
(305) 524-4052   FAX (305) 527-2600

Clients deserve environments of sanctuary for work and rest—with beauty and completeness realized as the sum of all design elements. Through collaboration, projects become an opportunity for fulfilling functional requirements with personal style, thus creating balance affecting all aspects of life.

Touching the human spirit, beauty is an expression of oneself guided by knowledge of and sensitivity to the aesthetic as well as human need. Personal expression is the key to creativity, achieving a definite objective by tapping the diverse resources of our planet, wherein no definition of individual style is limited to "traditional" or "contemporary". These terms simply identify specific items within one's personal domain. The result is comfortable, refined, poetic and timeless with great attention to quality and detail in both the furnishings and architectural appointments... Classic design with a new awareness for allowing the human spirit an extraordinary place to be nurtured and grow. To learn, to create and to reflect—in a word, to heal. ∎

PROJECTS:
Private Residences: Florida; Ohio; Michigan; California; Pennsylvania; and New York City.

Commercial Work: Restaurants, Executive Offices and Store and Yacht Design in Michigan, Florida, Ohio and California.

NANCY PICKARD INTERIORS

NANCY PICKARD HUMPHREY
1450 WOODLEY ROAD
MONTGOMERY, AL 36106
(205) 265-3974   FAX (205) 265-3974

PROJECTS:
Private Residences: Deer Valley and
Park City, Utah; New York, Amagansett
and Long Island, New York; Chicago,
Illinois; Fort Walton Beach and
Sandestin, Florida; and Montgomery and
the Alabama Gulf Coast.

Commercial Work: Luxury Residential
and Commercial Interiors for Model
Apartments, Clubhouses, Lobby Areas
and Sales Offices for Real Estate
Developers. Projects located in Baton
Rouge, Louisiana; Nashville, Tennessee;
Little Rock, Arkansas; Atlanta, Georgia;
Philadelphia, Pennsylvania; and Gulf
Shores, Alabama. Other commercial
commissions include: First Montgomery
Bank, Weil Brothers Cotton, Inc., The
Bistro and The Locker Room in
Montgomery, Alabama; and First
National Bank in Fort Walton Beach,
Florida.

CREDENTIALS:
Stratford College
21 years of experience in the design field
Founded Nancy Pickard Interiors in 1974

BELOW: Humphrey Residence in
Montgomery, Alabama

OPPOSITE, ABOVE LEFT: Nancy Pickard
Interiors

OPPOSITE, ABOVE RIGHT: Harmon
Residence in Montgomery, Alabama

OPPOSITE, BELOW: Williamson Residence
in Montgomery, Alabama

REBECCA

REBECCA STAHR
P.O. BOX 70952
MARIETTA, GA 30007
(404) 993-0310

■ *A trusting part-
nership between
client and designer
begins with thorough
communication and
confidence in one
another. This partner-
ship demystifies the
design process, makes
it more fun and creates
an ongoing relation-
ship that lasts the
course of time.*

*A designer's greatest
satisfaction is enabling
a client to discover
new dimensions of
ambiance in their per-
sonal world. Helping a
client to reach and live
their vision (be it in
a private or corporate
setting) while keeping
within a reasonable
budget, results in a
win/win project that
says it all.* ■

PROJECTS:
Private Residences: Atlanta and
Savannah, Georgia; New Orleans,
Louisiana; Destin, Florida; and San
Francisco, California.

Commercial Work: Corporate Offices
and Model Homes.

CREDENTIALS:
Louisiana State University, BS
Georgia State University, BVA
ASID, Allied Member
Who's Who in Interior Design, 1990, 1991
Freelance Design Writer
International Merchandising Buyer

PUBLISHED IN:
The Atlanta Journal & Constitution
Atlanta Homes and Lifestyles
Chattanooga News-Free Press
Know Atlanta
Presenting the Season
Peachtree

RILEY-BROWN, INC., INTERIOR DESIGNERS

PATTI RILEY-BROWN, ASID
4107 SPICEWOOD SPRINGS ROAD
SUITE 104
AUSTIN, TX 78759
(512) 795-8801   FAX (512) 795-8232

■ *It's important to incorporate the client's preferences and budget constraints into our firm's projects while utilizing solid professional training, as well as knowledge of construction and design talent, to perfect the outcome.* ■

PROJECTS:
Private Residences: London, England; Riyadh, Saudi Arabia; Baltimore, Maryland; Key Biscayne, Florida; Taos, New Mexico; Texarkana, Austin, Houston and various other Texas cities.

Commercial Work: College Housing: 14 states. Retail: various Texas cities. Hospitality: Cairo, Egypt; Austin, Texas; Matamoros and Guadalajara, Mexico. Institutions & Health Care: various Texas cities. Banks and Savings and Loans: various Texas cities.

CREDENTIALS:
University of Texas, B S Interior Design
Departmental Visiting Committee, University of Texas
University of Texas Distinguished Alumna, 1992
ASID, Professional Member
ASID, National, State and Local Board Member
ASID, Association Chair, 1992
ASID, Medalist of Society, 1988
ASID, Design Excellence Award, 1985
Texas Association for Interior Designers (TAID), Member
TAID, Board of Directors
John Tryon Robinson Award, 1992 (TAID)
Women in Construction
Illuminating Engineering Society
International Furnishings & Design Association
Applied for registration with Texas Board of Architectural Examiners, 1992

PUBLISHED IN:
Designers West
Interior Design
Southern Living
Texas Homes
Austin Homes & Gardens
Various banking and builders publications

ABOVE OPPOSITE: Formal dining room vignette incorporating square glass table to seat eight and infinite accessory detail.

BELOW OPPOSITE: Family room incorporating elegance of existing historical house with practical and usable finishes and appointments, and custom cabinetry.

ABOVE: Casual sun room for entertaining and family use.

SANTI'S INTERIORS, INC.

SANTIAGO MIRANDA
260 CRANDON BOULEVARD, #38
KEY BISCAYNE VILLA, FL 33149
(305) 361-7990

■ *I've practiced design in Europe and the Americas since my tutelage under Morris Lapidus 26 years ago. Primarily, I study my client's psycho/social environment and try to use time expeditiously with care and enthusiasm. My Cuban heritage has given me a great appreciation for European art and antiques which I specify according to my clients' desires as a timeless investment for generations to come.* ■

PROJECTS:
Private Residences: Paris; Spain; Costa Rica; Honduras; Colombia; Ecuador; Dominican Republic; Venezuela; Guatemala; Houston, Texas; Delaware; New York; and Florida.

CREDENTIALS:
ASID, Allied
Florida State License #196
Annual Continuing Education
  Courses, CEIDG

PUBLISHED IN:
Florida Designers Quarterly
Vanidades
Numerous Local Publications

ABOVE: Eclecticism is reflected with the use of period and traditional pieces from the Ming Dynasty mirror to the La Lique and Bacarat collection.

BELOW: The outdoor environment is integrated into the dining area with a palette of rose, green straw and lacquer, embellished with a formal tassel—that's Florida! Casual with formal overtones.

OPPOSITE: This entertainment area is euphonious with sound and past cultures. The art is an investment as well as an expression of emotion.

SEG INTERIORS, INC.

MARGARET CHAMBERS, ASID
2719 LACLEDE, SUITE B
DALLAS, TX 75204
(214) 871-9222 FAX (214) 871-0644

■ *My commitment to clients is to listen —listen to their dreams and visions of what they desire in a home or office. I work within a broad range of styles, but no matter the style, my goal is to create comfortable and visually pleasing interiors that reflect the owner's personality.* ■

PROJECTS:
Private Residences: Dallas; New York; and St. Louis, Missouri. References available upon request.

Commercial Work: Dallas, San Antonio, Houston and Vicksburg. References available upon request.

CREDENTIALS:
ASID, Professional Member
ASID, Dallas Association Chairman, 1989
ASID, Texas Chapter Board Member, 1989-1992
El Centro College, Interior Design
New Mexico State University, Fine Arts
Parson European Studies, Italy
Educational Study, China
Design Ovation Award, ASID Honorable Mention, Entry/Showhouse, 1991
March of Dimes Gourmet Gala Design Chairman, 1988-89
Beaux Arts Ball, DMA, Decorative Arts Committee, Co-Chairman, 1991
Designers West Top 10 Designers, 1989

PUBLISHED IN:
Designers West
Traditional Home
Window & Wall
Dallas Times Herald
Builder/Architect

ABOVE: Fantasy Nursery - Antique Victorian iron crib, handmade and painted French doll house, whimsical handmade and painted bunny chair, antique dolls and silver frame collection.

LEFT: Room With a View - all upholstery custom designed and built, eclectic mixture of antiques and styles.

JOHN PHIFER MARRS, ASID
2719 LACLEDE, SUITE C
DALLAS, TX 75204
(214) 871-9753   FAX (214) 871-0644

■ *In today's world
it is very impor-
tant to be surrounded
by beauty, harmony
and order in the rooms
where we live and
work. My goal as an
interior designer is to
gently guide the client
to this serene environ-*
*ment that usually
only the designer sees
at the project's begin-
ning, but hopefully
everyone appreciates
at the end.* ■

PROJECTS:
Private Residences: References available
upon request.

Commercial Work: Corporate Executive
offices and Home Furnishing
Showrooms.

CREDENTIALS:
ASID, Professional Member
ASID, Texas Chapter President, 1991-92

PUBLISHED IN:
Traditional Home
Window & Wall
Designers West
Designers World
Dallas Morning News
Dallas Times Herald

RIGHT: Antique furniture and accessories
enhance the entry of a Dallas residence.

BELOW: Comfort balances with elegance
in this colorful living area.

JIMMY SELLARS, INTERIOR DECORATION

JAMES E. SELLARS
1827 RIDGE AVENUE
MONTGOMERY, AL 36106
(205) 265-0038

Mr. Sellars' intuitive sense of design and style combines with an in-depth knowledge of color and scale to create interiors for residences ranging from English townhouses to seaside cottages in the sunny South, each distinctively unique.

A classicist in design, he uses traditionalism as a point of departure to create an atmosphere reflecting a client's individuality and lifestyle. The meticulous selection of fabrics, furnishings and paintings reflects Mr. Sellars' absolute attention to detail, an unerring eye for quality and a passion for the extraordinary.

PROJECTS:
Private Residences: Montgomery, Alabama; Seaside, Florida; London, England; Cannes, France; and Cairo and Alexandria, Egypt.

CREDENTIALS:
Huntington College
Auburn University, BA, 1965
Auburn University, MFA, 1972
Film and Television Set Decoration, 1965-73

PUBLISHED IN:
Art and Decoration, 9/86, 2/87
House and Garden, Britain, 2/92, 5/92
Veranda, Winter 1992

THIS PAGE AND OPPOSITE ABOVE:
Maghraby Residence in London, England

OPPOSITE BELOW: Newell Residence in Montgomery, Alabama

SCOTT SNYDER, INC.

SCOTT SNYDER
99 VIA MIZNER-WORTH AVENUE
PALM BEACH, FL 33480
(407) 659-6255   FAX (407) 832-5946

■ *A respect for architectural preservation with strong ties to classicism are the traditions which we at Scott Snyder, Inc. bring to our work. Our success has come from working closely with our clients to create elegance in every nuance of design. As a full-service firm, we are able to meet every need in architecture, space planning and interior design.* ■

PROJECTS:
Private Residences: Palm Beach, Boca Raton and Miami, Florida; Dallas, Texas; Greenwich, Connecticut; and Beaver Creek, Colorado.

CREDENTIALS:
14+ years of experience in design
Owner of upscale home furnishings store offering expert design services

Owner of full-service interior design firm with retail shop since 1984
Extensive world travel

PUBLISHED IN:
Southern Accents
W Magazine
Thai House and Garden
Palm Beach Life
Palm Beach Illustrated

PHOTOS: A recently published Designer's Showhouse, "Casa Del Asilo": The 19th century neoclassic statues, combined with the carefully selected lighting and English-inspired floral arrangements, set the mood for dining. The murals allow your mind to wander beyond the parameter of the room. Fabrics by Scalamandre, English antiques from Kentshire Galleries,

New York; floral arrangements by "Gardenstyle"—another Scott Snyder venture.

EDWARD H. SPRINGS INTERIORS, INC.

EDWARD H. SPRINGS, ASID
1236 E. MOREHEAD STREET
CHARLOTTE, NC 28204
(704) 376-6461   FAX (704) 343-0651

■ *Listening to our clients' needs, interpreting their wishes and encouraging them to stretch artistically to arrive at a design solution that is aesthetically exciting and, above all, suitable for their lifestyle—that is our design philosophy.* ■

PROJECTS:
Private Residences: Atherton, California; Houston, Texas; Horton Bay, Michigan; Boca Raton, Florida; and Princeton, New Jersey.

Commercial Work: Sonoco World Headquarters, Hartsville, South Carolina; Bascom Palmer Eye Institute, Miami, Florida; and Charlotte Plastic Surgery, Charlotte, North Carolina.

CREDENTIALS:
Ringling School of Art, Sarasota, Florida
ASID, Professional Member

PUBLISHED IN:
Southern Accents
House Beautiful
Interiors
Interior Design
Colonial Homes
Traditional Home

COMPENSATION/FEE STRUCTURE:
Residential: Retail
Contract: Design Fee/Hourly Rate

ABOVE LEFT: Reminiscent of state beds in the grandest of country homes in England and France, the intricately carved Chippendale poster bed makes a commanding performance in this guest room.

BELOW LEFT: Assured selectivity has appointed this classic room in the Nouveau idiom. Sparkling colors grounded in aquamarine, create a veritable jewel box.

OPPOSITE: This dining room reflects the timeless appeal of classic decorating devices. Furnishings are chosen from popular revival styles and the white marble floor is a perfect foil for the scheme.

SHARON STALEY INTERIORS

SHARON STALEY, ASID
5320 GULFTON, SUITE 6
HOUSTON, TX 77081
(713) 668-9689 FAX (713) 668-8307

■ *I believe that good design starts and ends by accurately reflecting the client's needs into a workable and comfortable living space. I encourage my client's participation in the design process because it builds the trust and understanding needed to create timeless, classic spaces.*

A high degree of integrity and professionalism coupled with cost efficiency and good listening skills have made it possible for me to provide my clients with the detail and personal service so necessary to achieving good creative design goals. ■

PROJECTS:
Private Residences: Texas and Louisiana.

Commercial Work: Hotels; Decor Offices; and Executive Offices in the Houston area.

CREDENTIALS:
Texas Tech University
ASID, Texas Gulf Coast Chapter President
Who's Who in Interior Design

PUBLISHED IN:
Houston Home and Garden
Houston Living
Houston Chronicle
Builder/Architect Magazine
Houston Remodeling and Design
Houston Post

CARL STEELE ASSOCIATES, INC.

CARL STEELE
1606 PINE STREET
PHILADELPHIA, PA 19103
(215) 546-5530 FAX (215) 546-1571

■ *A room should be aesthetically pleasing and at the same time functional. The individual touches above the basics of furniture, fabrics and color give the room its special character and make it complete.* ■

PROJECTS:
Private Residences: Philadelphia, Pennsylvania; New York; and Florida.

Commercial Work: Corporate Law Offices; Subaru of America Executive Office; Super Box; Philadelphia Stadium; and Private Yachts.

CREDENTIALS:
ASID
Philadelphia—University of the Arts
Philadelphia Designer of the Year

PUBLISHED IN:
Fairchild Publications
Town & Country
The New York Times
House Beautiful
Philadelphia Magazine
Philadelphia Inquirer

JoyCe Stolberg Interiors, Inc.

JOYCE STOLBERG
2205 NE 207TH STREET
NORTH MIAMI BEACH, FL 33180
(305) 931-6010   FAX (305) 931-6040

■ *Residentially, my relationship with each client is relaxed and informal. Some of my best friends are clients! I prefer to install the entire concept, focusing on aesthetics and longevity because the client will have a long term relationship with their environment.*

On a commercial basis, I concentrate on the company's product, service or image, and then I try to balance that with the client's artistic sense. ■

PROJECTS:
Private Residences: Florida; Michigan; New York; Canada; Panama; England; and Israel.

Commercial Work: In Florida—Pratesi Showhouse, Miami Beach; Sheraton Hotel, Dania; Vacation Break USA; Time Shares; Restaurants; Offices; Medical Centers; Models; and Beauty Salons. In the Caribbean—Hotels.

CREDENTIALS:
ISID, Member
 International Furnishing and
 Design Association, Member
IDG, Member
Designer of the Year Awards,
 Special Area, 1980
Designer of the Year Awards, Residential,
 Limited Budget, 1980, 1990
Designer of the Year Awards, Turnberry
 Isle Beauty Salon, 1981
"Ardy" Award Nominee,
 Coconut Bay Resort, 1992

PUBLISHED IN:
Southern Accents
The Designer
Design South
On Design
IDEAS Magazine
Florida Designers Quarterly
Florida Builders
Miami Magazine
Vanidades/Decoration & Casa
Florida Home Furnishings
World of Turnberry
Miami South Florida
Miami Summer Boat Show Guide
Interior Design & Home Furnishings Guide

ABOVE: Residence at Williams Island

LEFT: Turnberry Isle Beauty Salon

OPPOSITE: "The Royal Nursery" for the ISID Pratesi Showhouse

Stone-Vining Design Associates

CYNTHIA STONE
DONNA VINING
3920 WESTHEIMER, SUITE F
HOUSTON, TX 77027
(713) 623-4061   FAX (713) 623-2573

■ *Our goal for each project is to accurately express our client's individual tastes. We hope that each project is unique from others and is a true reflection of our client's lifestyle. Our most successful interiors have evolved from a close working relationship and exchange of ideas with our clients. When we hear "we had a great time and we love everything," then our job is complete.* ■

PROJECTS:
Private Residences: Houston, Dallas, Beaumont, San Antonio, and Austin, Texas; Tucson, Arizona; Aspen, Colorado; Baltimore, Maryland; Boston, Massachusetts; New Orleans, Louisiana; Ft. Lauderdale, Florida; New York City; Saudi Arabia; Japan; and Mexico.

Commercial Work: Wiltel Corporate Offices; Parkway Hotel–Disney World; St. Luke's Hospital; Texas Children's Hospital; Texas Heart Institute; Hermann Hospital; University of Texas Health Science Center; Baylor College of Medicine; St. Joseph Professional Building; Texas Air Systems Corporate Office; and Garrett Petrochemical Corporate Office.

CREDENTIALS:
CYNTHIA STONE:
  ASID, Allied Member
  GHBA/HAA/ROBWEC

DONNA VINING:
  ASID
  GHBA/HAA/ROBWEC

ASID Designer Showhouse, 1988, 1992
Zeta Tau Alpha Showhouse, 1980, 1981, 1985
March of Dimes 1980, 1981, 1987, 1988

Street of Dreams Award Winner,
  Sweetwater, 1988
  Clear Lake, 1989
  Northgate, 1990
Beaumont Mental Health Showcase, 1990
Festival of Trees "Best of Show," 1990
Texas Homes Showcase, 1990
Houston Junior League
  "A Taste of Elegance," 1988
Celebrity Paws Gala, 1991
Brookwood Community
  "Street of Sante Fe," 1988

PUBLISHED IN:
Houston Home and Garden
Ultra
Texas Homes
Houston Metropolitan
The Black Book
Creative Ideas for Living
Pinnacle
Houston Post
Houston Chronicle

PAT STOTLER INTERIORS, INC.

PAT STOTLER
110 CORAL CAY DRIVE
PALM BEACH GARDENS, FL 33418
(407) 627-0527   FAX (407) 626-7015

■ *As designers we are dedicated to providing timeless interiors, thus creating an environment that clients may enjoy for many years to come. We work in partnership with our clients to ensure an end result reflective of their tastes, one that meets the needs of their current lifestyle and represents fine design as well.*

We believe it is important to proceed at a comfortable pace and, above all, we endeavor to make the entire experience pleasurable and personally rewarding for both client and designer. ■

PROJECTS:
Private Residences: South Florida;
Cincinnati, Ohio; and Houston, Texas.

CREDENTIALS:
Westchester College, BS
Syracuse University, MS
Lighthouse Gallery Showcase Houses,
 1991, 1992

PUBLISHED IN:
Palm Beach Illustrated
Focus Magazine
Miami Herald
Indian River Pictorial
Palm Beach Post
Palm Beach County Visitors Guide
Guide to Martin County

Thrasher Design Company, Inc.

JEFFREY THRASHER
CORAL GABLES, FL 33114
(305) 445-5914   FAX (305) 446-9989

■ *Carefully chosen details, natural beauty and pure craftsmanship are classic — clean, simple design is also timeless. Environments should reflect the interests and tastes of the people who live there, as well as where they live, their climate,*

the tone of light. I emphasize the innate, natural beauty of objects—a line, a grain, a polish, a color. ■

PROJECTS:
Private Residences: South Florida; New York; Central and South America; and Vail, Colorado.

Commercial Work:
Coral Gables, Florida

CREDENTIALS:
ASID
University of Kentucky,
  BA, Interior Design
Florida State License #2501
Designers Showhouse benefitting the
  Children's Home Society
Designer Showhouse benefitting the
  New World Symphony

PUBLISHED IN:
Interiors
South Florida Home & Garden
The Post Newspaper, Florida

LEFT: Commissioned mural of South Miami Beach by Michael Abrams, New York. Private residence, Williams Island, Florida.

BELOW AND OPPOSITE: A notable collection of Hagenauer figures in bronze and nickel.

SANDI TICKNER INTERIORS

SANDI TICKNER
20424 NE 16TH PLACE
NORTH MIAMI BEACH, FL 33179
(305) 653-1190 FAX (305) 654-8898

I love my work and enjoy working with my clients. It is important to me that my clients are happy and comfortable with the results. In my initial interviews with prospective clients, I allow time

to get to know their personalities and their individuality. We shop together so that there is no question as to the design, color and feel of what they most desire. Regardless of budget constraints, there is always room for individual creativity. ■

PROJECTS:
Private Residences: Florida; New York; New Jersey; St. Thomas, Virgin Islands; Montego Bay, Jamaica; Grand Cayman Islands; Nassau, Bahamas; and Bogotá, Colombia.

Commercial Work: Executive Offices in Banco De Caldas and Bogotá, Colombia; ICL Corporation in Delray Beach, Florida; Inteuro Auto Parts in Miami, Tampa and Jacksonville, Florida; and International Intimates on Madison Avenue in New York City.

CREDENTIALS:
Interior Design Guild
IDG Showcase House

DOROTHY H. TRAVIS INTERIORS, INC.

DOROTHY H. TRAVIS
12 KINGS CIRCLE NE
ATLANTA, GA 30305
(404) 233-7207 FAX (404) 233-7260

■ *My goal is to interpret the tastes and desires of my clients and create timeless interiors suitable to their life-styles. The intent is to create a comfortable, relaxed environment, blending antiques and contemporary pieces. I have a reverence for the past and a passion for the new—with criteria based on the very best in quality, proper proportions and aesthetic beauty.* ■

PROJECTS:
Private Residences: Atlanta, Sea Island, Macon, Columbus, Savannah and various other homes in Georgia; Greensboro, Mount Airy, Rutherfordton, High Point, Durham and various homes along the coast of North Carolina; Charlottesville, Virginia; Washington, D.C.; New York City; Sante Fe, New Mexico; Harbor Springs, Michigan; Coastal Maine; and Jackson, Mississippi.

Commercial Work: Greensboro Country Club in Greensboro, North Carolina; Corporate Law and Insurance Firms in Atlanta, Georgia; and Major Medical and Dental Offices.

CREDENTIALS:
ISID

PUBLISHED IN:
Southern Accents
Veranda
Southern Homes

RICHARD TRIMBLE & ASSOCIATES, INC.

RICHARD TRIMBLE
6517 HILLCREST, SUITE 409
DALLAS, TX 75205
(214) 363-2283   FAX (214) 363-2283

What is important to me are my clients' wishes, and interpreting them into an aesthetically pleasing design without sacrificing function and personal comfort. Rapport and trust between client and designer are essential, especially in residential design which is such a personal statement.

Many of my clients have been with me since I started the firm— some through multiple residences and offices, others implementing a master plan step by step. ■

PROJECTS:
Private Residences: Dallas, San Antonio
and Marshall, Texas; Big Sky, Montana;
Charlottesville, Virginia; Chicago, Illinois;
and Mobile, Alabama.

Commercial Work: Executive Offices,
Board Rooms, Conference Spaces, Legal
and Medical Offices and Banks.

CREDENTIALS:
Marketing, BBA
Interior Design, BFA
Master of Arts Degree
Oxford-Worcester College, English
  Country House Program
ASID, Allied Member
Dallas Symphony Showhouse
Kappa Alpha Theta Designer Showhouse
16 years of design experience
Licensed designer—Texas

PUBLISHED IN:
Southern Living
Dallas—Fort Worth Home &
  Garden
Texas Homes
Better Homes & Gardens —
  Traditional Homes
Decorating with Southern Living
Dallas Life
Dallas Morning News
Dallas Times Herald

RICKI TUCKER INTERIORS AND CABIN ANTIQUES

RICKI TUCKER
ROUTE 8, BOX 109
MERIDIAN, MS 39305
(601) 679-7921

A good designer should be able to interpret a client's personality, lifestyle and taste, and incorporate them into the client's interiors. However, after the basic elements of good design are achieved, accessories play a vital role in completing the decor.

No room looks complete until the paintings, pillows, flowers, plants, and personal collections are in place. They are the most useful tools in converting a "house" into a comfortable, welcoming and well-loved "home". ∎

PROJECTS:
Private Residences: Mississippi and Alabama.

CREDENTIALS:
Mississippi College, BA
Inchbald School, London
Practical experience in home interior design

PUBLISHED IN:
Southern Accents
Mississippi Magazine

VanTosh & Associates

JILL VANTOSH
1479 SPRING STREET
ATLANTA, GA 30309
(404) 881-6074 FAX (404) 888-0613

■ *Interpreting today's lifestyles demands an awareness of our clients' needs. My goal is to create a harmony within by combining aesthetics with personality and function. I like to punctuate my spaces with my clients rare treasures, classical elements and original works of art, creating a timelessness melded with the comforts of today's world.*

With 20 years of design experience, my clients can utilize our services from the threshold of conception to the unfolding of the finished product. Whatever phase we begin our relationship, it is paramount that each design set a stage that best reflects the image of the client. ■

PROJECTS:
Private Residences: Atlanta, Georgia and Suburbs; Bal Harbour and Long Boat Key, Florida; Montgomery, Alabama; and Knoxville, Tennessee.

Commercial Work: Executive, Corporate, Medical and Legal Offices; Retail Space; Showrooms; Restaurants; Vacation Lodges; Model Homes; Residential Lobbies and Public Space in Atlanta, Georgia and Suburbs; Athens, Georgia; Nashville, Tennessee; Charlotte and Winston-Salem, North Carolina; Dallas, Texas; and Kansas City, Missouri.

CREDENTIALS:
University of Georgia, BA
ISID
Art Institute of Atlanta, Faculty Member
Seminars and Local Groups, Speaker
Historic Preservation Award
Atlanta Home Festival Design Awards 1989-1991—Benefit Scottish Rite Hospital
American Crafts Show Vignette 1990-1991—Benefit Georgia Trust for Historic Preservation
Tour of Homes, 1985
Model Housing Awards—National and Local

PUBLISHED IN:
Atlanta Magazine
Atlanta Journal
Better Homes and Gardens (cover)
Southern Homes (cover)
Woman's Day
Real Estate Investor (cover)
Atlanta Homes
Condominiums Magazine
Atlanta Homes and Lifestyles
Peachtree Magazine
Better Homes and Gardens Home Plan Ideas (cover)

MICHAEL VON ZURHORST INTERIORS

MICHAEL VON ZURHORST
916 CLINT MOORE ROAD
BOCA RATON, FL 33487
(407) 241-4705

■ *To design is to materialize in time and space and form and color and texture, a mirrored image of the client's soul and personality; to externalize the existence and feeling from within to an expression of essence and lifestyle tempered with practicality, balance and classic taste.* ■

PROJECTS:
Residential and Commercial work:
Bloomfield Development, St. Andrew's
Country Club, The Polo Club, Broken Sound
Country Club, Mizner Tower, Boca West,
Les Jardin and Boca Pointe, Boca Raton,
Florida; PGA National and Admiral's Cove,
Palm Beach, Florida; Bal Harbour Tower,
Bal Harbour, Florida; and Key West, Florida.

CREDENTIALS:
Bauder College, 1984
Showcase House Coral Gables, 1992

PUBLISHED IN:
Florida Home & Garden, February 1990;
 April 1990, cover

FRANYA WAIDE ANTIQUES AND INTERIORS

FRANYA WAIDE, ASID
2300 PEACHTREE ROAD, SUITE B-103
ATLANTA, GA 30309
(404) 352-2300   FAX (404) 352-4510

■ *Our philosophy is based on the conviction that successful design must blend the finest antique pieces with today's contemporary furnishings, if we are to create a home of elegance and comfort, blended with a sense of history and romance.*

We are mindful that an understanding of the client's particular style is critical to a successful project.

Franya Waide is known to shop internationally (England, France, Argentina) for fine French and English 18th and 19th century antique pieces for clients, as well as for her well established antique shop. ■

PROJECTS:
Private Residences: Georgia; Connecticut; Illinois; Texas; Alabama; Florida; Tennessee; and California.

Commercial Work: Georgia

CREDENTIALS:
Auburn University
ASID
International Furnishings and Design
   Association
Baron's Who's Who in Interior Design,
   International Edition

PUBLISHED IN:
Town & Country
Southern Homes
Atlanta Magazine
Interior Design
Atlanta Journal & Constitution
Presenting the Season

MARIE WARREN INTERIORS

MARIE WARREN
349 PEACHTREE HILLS AVENUE
ATLANTA, GA 30305
(404) 231-0630

When I walk into a room I did 25 years ago and feel that it is still right for my client, I know I have succeeded.

My great fear is to overhear someone say, "that looks like a Marie Warren room." I have tried to avoid having a special stamp. After all, if no two people are the same, then neither should be their surroundings. When my clients are at home alone, reading, relaxing or just doing their daily routines, they must feel content with the surroundings. That's what it's all about. ■

PROJECTS:
Private Residences: Atlanta, Duluth
Sea Island and Waycross, Georgia;
Birmingham, Alabama; Charleston, South
Carolina; Manhattan; East Hampton,
New York; Lookout Mountain,
Tennessee; Naples, Florida; Tiburon,
California; and Tryon, North Carolina.

PUBLISHED IN:
Architectural Digest
Veranda
Southern Homes
Florida Architecture
Atlanta Journal Magazine

J. WESTERFIELD ANTIQUES & INTERIORS, INC.

JIM WESTERFIELD
4429 OLD CANTON ROAD
JACKSON, MS 39211
(601) 362-7508   FAX (601) 366-4718

■ *With 33 years of decorating experience, Jim Westerfield creates timeless interiors which express his clients' unique personalities. His expertise in selecting quality period furnishings results in excellent investments for the homeowner. Using master craftsmen to construct handmade cabinetry, he stresses the paramount importance of detail.* ■

PROJECTS:
Private Residences: Mississippi; Montgomery and Birmingham, Alabama; Dallas, Texas; Los Angeles, California; Sea Island, Georgia; and St. Petersburg and Long Boat Key, Florida.

Commercial Work: Executive and Law Offices; Restaurants; Retail Shops; Hotels; Country Clubs; and Yachts in Mississippi, Alabama, Tennessee and Texas.

CREDENTIALS:
Millsaps College
New York School of Interior Design
ASID, Affiliate

PUBLISHED IN:
Veranda
Architectural Digest
Interior Design
The Designer Specifier
The Los Angeles Times
The SUNDAY Tennessean

CATHY WHITLOCK, INC.

CATHY WHITLOCK
3384 JOFFRE PLACE
MEMPHIS, TN 38111
(901) 454-6083

■ *I follow the late designer Billy Baldwin's axiom, "Nothing is in good taste unless it suits the way you live. What is practical is beautiful, and suitability always overrules fashion."*

My work is influenced by the European attitude towards interiors that reflect an easy, understated elegance and a sophisticated use of color, combined with an architectural feel and unexpected touch of the whimsical.

As a designer, my goal is to create rooms that make a statement about the tastes and lifestyles of the people who live there, while complying with their budget. Interior decoration should be a collaborative effort.

Most importantly, I try to remember one golden rule of decorating—rules are made to be broken!■

PROJECTS:
Private Residences: New York City, Rye, Scarsdale and Brooklyn Heights, New York; Greenwich, Connecticut; Chicago, Lake Forest and Lake Bluff, Illinois; Philadelphia, Pennsylvania; Los Angeles, California; and Memphis and Tullahoma, Tennessee.

Commercial Work: Various Offices in New York.

CREDENTIALS:
Parsons School of Design, New York
ASID

PUBLISHED IN:
Town & Country

GAIL BRINN WILKINS, INC.

GAIL BRINN WILKINS
600 QUEENS ROAD
CHARLOTTE, NC 28207
(704) 376-2651   FAX (704) 333-7310

■ *The art of living is very personal. Through excellent craftsmanship, creativity, love for tradition, sound quality, professional procedures and a sincere magical sense of innovation, we at Gail Brinn Wilkins Interiors ensure this truth. By listening to*

and interpreting the client's desires, the design process unfolds, blending roots of yesterday, a lot of today's lifestyles and a hint of tomorrow. We allow people to be all they can be in this very personal endeavor. Residential and commercial clients both find this process essential for today's living and working environments. ■

PROJECTS:
Private Residences: Chapel Hill, Figure Eight Island, Asheville, Hickory, Fayetteville and Charlotte, North Carolina; Olympia, Washington; Tampa, Florida; New York City; and Debordieu, South Carolina.

Commercial Work: Bill Nessen Showroom in the Dacota Center in Dania, Florida; Stanley Knitting Mills Executive Offices in New York City. In North Carolina: The Orchid Shop in Charlotte; Charlotte Convention Center, Visitors Offices and Meeting Rooms; Jack Winslow, DDS in Rocky Mount; Carolina Trace Country Club in Sanford; Governor's Club Cottages in Chapel Hill; Chesson Realty Company in Durham; and A. Marshall Basinger, Esq. Law Offices in Charlotte.

CREDENTIALS:
New York School of Interior Design
Musee Des Arts Decoratifs, Parsons
 School of Design, Paris, France
ASID, Professional Member
ASID Designer of the Year,
 Carolina's Chapter
ASID Showhouse Design Award,
 Carolina's Chapter
Who's Who in Interior Design
Mint Museum of Art Home and Garden
 Selection 1972, 1988
Design-In-Excellence Awards,
 Presentation Speaker
Interior Design Magazine Symposium,
 Speaker, Design ADAC Atlanta
International Furnishings and Design
 Association
National Association of Home Builders
Charlotte Homebuilders Association
National Women of the Arts, North
 Carolina Board
National Historic Preservation Society

PUBLISHED IN:
Design South
CITI Magazine
Southern Accents
Health Today
The Charlotte Observer
Southern Living
Furniture Today
North Carolina Homes & Gardens
Business Properties
Charlotte Magazine

YOUNG & COMPANY

JAMES BOYD YOUNG
125 5TH STREET NE
ATLANTA, GA 30308
(404) 875-8048   FAX (404) 874-2422

P.O. BOX 2022
HOBE SOUND, FL 33475
(407) 546-8392

PROJECTS:
Private Residences Throughout the
United States.

Commercial Work: Atlanta Athletic Club
Country Club; Highland Country Club;
Emory University; and Piedmont
Hospitals.

CREDENTIALS:
University of Georgia, Business
  Administration
Parsons School of Design, New York
Atlanta Decorative Arts Center Hall of
  Fame, 1992
Atlanta Decorative Arts Center Interior
  Designer of the Year, 1987
Hexter Award
25 years of interior design
  experience

PUBLISHED IN:
Southern Accents
Southern Homes
Veranda
Design South
HG

ABOVE: French and English influence
for a seasonal house in Florida.

BELOW: Part of a collection of historical
equestrian paintings assembled in the
main house of a Kentucky horse farm.

OPPOSITE: Side niches created to give
scale and balance to a Florida living
room. Linen and silk against the colors
of a pool.

TOBY ZACK DESIGNS, INC.

TOBY ZACK
3201 GRIFFIN ROAD, SUITE 204
FT. LAUDERDALE, FL 33312
(305) 967-8629   FAX (305) 981-5384

■ *My success comes from designing interiors with the priority of function based on the needs of each client. The uniqueness of my design is timeless, clean and understated. My special ability is to cohesively mix design concepts with artistic creations.* ■

PROJECTS:
Private Residences: Renovation and restoration of 1920 home in Miami, Florida; residential design for private residences located throughout the United States, especially Florida and Michigan; design projects also in Canada and Switzerland.

Commercial Work: Florida yacht and boat interior design; office design for Price Waterhouse; art gallery design for Zack/Schuster Galleries.

CREDENTIALS:
ISID
IDG
Boston University, BA
Who's Who in Interior Design
IDG Designer of the Year Award,
   1982, 1983, 1984, 1985
American Red Cross Designers' Showhouse
FAME Award Winner for Outstanding
   Interior Design

PUBLISHED IN:
Metropolitan Home
Interior Design
The Designer/Specifier
South Florida Home and Garden
FDQ Design South, cover
Palm Beach Life Magazine
Boca Raton Magazine
Palm Beach Post
Palm Beach Daily News

INDEX OF INTERIOR DESIGNERS

A & I PLACE/ANTIQUES &
INTERIORS, THE
26-27

AMBIANCE INTERIORS
28-29

AQUINO INTERIORS, CLAUDIA
30-31

ARELLANO INTERIORS, INC., MARIO
32-33
■

BARBER, INC., GINGER
34-35

BERENSON INTERIOR DESIGN, INC.,
JOHN
36-37

BLADES/MICHAEL'S ANTIQUES,
KATRINA
38-39

BRANCH AND ASSOCIATES,
RICHARD
40-43

BRITO INTERIOR DESIGN, INC.
44-45

BROWNS INTERIORS, INC.
46-47

BRYAN DESIGN ASSOCIATES, THE
48-49
■

CARITHERS, DAN
50-51

CARRAGHER INTERIORS, INC.,
PAULETTE
52-53

CARSON INTERIOR DESIGN,
PATRICIA M.
54-55

CATAO & ASSOCIATES, INC.,
LOURDES
56-57

CHARLOTTE'S, INC.
58-59

COULSON-HAMLIN
60-61

COVINGTON DESIGN
ASSOCIATES, INC.
62-65

CRAFT INTERIORS, JOHN
66-67

CRAIG INTERIORS, N.
68-69
■

DAYVAULT & ASSOCIATES, J.
70-71

DESIGNERS UNLIMITED, INC.
72-73

DRAPER & ASSOCIATES, PAUL
74-75

DRUMMOND INTERIOR DESIGN,
GILLIAN
76-77
■

EDE, FASID, ARLIS
78-79

ELLIS, INC., STANLEY
80-81

ESSARY ASSOCIATES, INC., JAMES
82-83

EUBANKS INTERIOR DESIGN,
WILLIAM R.
84-87

EVANS INTERIORS, INC., AL
88-89
■

FETZER'S INTERIORS & FINE
ANTIQUES
90-91

FISHER INTERIORS, LIZ
92-93

FRANCIS DESIGN/DECORATION,
BILLY W.
94-97
■

GANDY/PEACE, INC.
98-99

GARDNER INTERIORS, LANDY
100-101

GRUBBS, INC., C. SMITH
102-103

GUYTON INTERIORS, KATHY
104-105
■

HAIM, FLINT & ASSOCIATES
106-107

HARMAN/THE
CORNER CUPBOARD ANTIQUES
AND INTERIORS, KATHERINE
108-109

HIMMEL, RICHARD
110-111

HOLCOMB INTERIORS, DAVID
112-113

HOLLEY, INC., RICHARD
114-115

HOWARD DESIGN, INC., J/
116-117
■

IDOL DESIGN, ROBERT
118-119

INTERIOR DESIGN GROUP, INC.
120-121
■

JOHNSTON INTERIORS, CHIP
122-123

BENJAMIN JONES, L.
124-125

JULIAN INTERIORS, INC., RUTH GRAY
126-127
■

CAROL KLOTZ INTERIORS/
REGALO ANTIQUES
128-129

KUCKLY ASSOCIATES, INC., MARTIN
130-133

KUHL DESIGN ASSOCIATES
134-135
■

LA MAISON FLEURIE, C.A.
136-137

LAPELLE INTERIORS, SUSAN
138-139

LARISCY, INC., R. WARD
140-141

LEET, INC.
142-143

LEHMAN INTERIORS, IRENE
144-145

LEONARD INTERIORS, JEANNE
146-147

GORDON LITTLE INTERIORS, T.
148-149

LUYK DESIGNS, INC., TON
150-151
■

MALE ASID, INC., JUDY R.
152-153

MANSOUR, MARIE
154-155

MARCUS ASSOCIATES, INC., ALLAN
DAVID
156-157

MARSDEN ANTIQUES & INTERIORS,
INC., JANE J.
158-159

McALPIN INTERIORS, INC., CLIFFORD
STILES
160-161

McINTOSH & ASSOCIATES, GENE
162-163

MENZIES INTERIOR DESIGN,
RODGERS
164-165

M.L. SLOVACK DESIGN, INC.
166-167

MOTZEL-SANS ASSOCIATES
168-169
■

NICHOLSON INTERIORS
170-171
■

OETGEN DESIGN AND FINE
ANTIQUES, INC.
172-173
■

PAGE CREATIVE DESIGNS, INC., JANE
174-175

PANKRATZ INTERNATIONAL, INC.
176-177

PICKARD INTERIORS, NANCY
178-179
■

REBECCA
180-181

RILEY-BROWN, INC. INTERIOR
DESIGNERS
182-183
■

SANTI'S INTERIORS, INC.
184-185

SEG INTERIORS, INC.
186-187

SELLARS, INTERIOR DECORATION,
JIMMY
188-189

SNYDER, INC., SCOTT
190-191

SPRINGS INTERIORS, INC.,
EDWARD H.
192-193

STALEY INTERIORS, SHARON
194-195

STEELE ASSOCIATES, INC., CARL
196-197

STOLBERG INTERIORS, INC., JOYCE
198-199

STONE-VINING DESIGN ASSOCIATES
200-201

STOTLER INTERIORS, INC., PAT
202-203
■

THRASHER DESIGN COMPANY, INC.
204-205

TICKNER INTERIORS, SANDI
206-207

TRAVIS INTERIORS, INC.,
DOROTHY H.
208-209

TRIMBLE & ASSOCIATES, INC.,
RICHARD
210-211

TUCKER INTERIORS AND CABIN
ANTIQUES, RICKI
212-213
■

VANTOSH & ASSOCIATES
214-215

VON ZURHORST INTERIORS,
MICHAEL
216-217
■

WAIDE ANTIQUES & INTERIORS,
FRANYA
218-219

WARREN INTERIORS, MARIE
220-221

WESTERFIELD ANTIQUES &
INTERIORS, INC., J.
222-223

WHITLOCK, INC., CATHY
224-225

WILKINS, INC., GAIL BRINN
226-227
■

YOUNG & COMPANY
228-229
■

ZACK DESIGNS, INC., TOBY
230-231
■

INDEX OF PHOTOGRAPHERS

ABRAMS, GARY
108, 109

ARROW PHOTOGRAPHY
198 bottom
■

BAILEY, ROBERT
132 top left and right, 133

BARDAGJY, PAUL
171

BENSON, SETH
156, 157

BENZUR,
GABRIELE/ARCHITECTURAL
PHOTOGRAPHY
80, 81

BERNARD, TOM
196 top

BESWICK, PAUL G./BESWICK
INTERNATIONAL, INC.
28 top, 29, 67, 226 top

BOND, WARREN
162, 163

BOULEY, RAY/BOULEY
CREATIVE GROUP
112, 113

BRENNAN, FRAN
34, 35, 114 bottom, 115, 134, 135

BROOK, STEVEN
150, 151 top

BURRELL, DELOY
128 top
■

CUNNINGHAM, DAN
104 bottom
■

DAVIS, JUDY
140 top, 141

DOBBS, RON E.
90 bottom

DOGGRELL, FRANCES
224 top, 225

DOMENECH, CARLOS
36 top, 106, 107, 120, 121,
151 bottom

DOW, LESLIE WRIGHT
13, 46, 47, 227

DURHAM, DAVID
160 bottom
■

ESPONDA PHOTOGRAPHY
182 top
■

FORD, GIL
222, 223

FORER, DAN/FORER, INC.
72, 73, 88, 89, 104 top, 116, 117,
144, 145, 176, 177, 197, 198 top,
199, 204, 205, 216, 217, 230 top,
231

FREEMAN, TINA
84,* 85,* 86 bottom*
* Property of Southern Accents

FREY PHOTOGRAPHY, FRED
91
■

GARBARINO, ALEXA
152, 153

GARDNER, JACK
180 bottom, 181

GARDNER, RICK
154, 155

GRESHAM, WALTER V. III
26 TOP

GRIFFETH STUDIO, DOT
172, 173

GROSSMAN, BARRY J./GROSSMAN
PHOTOGRAPHY
131, 184, 185, 206, 207

GRUNKE, JOHN
53, 124 TOP, 125, 180 TOP

GUERRERO, RAMON
44, 45
■

HART, NEIL
118 BOTTOM

HELFER, MARTIN
70

HICKEY-ROBERTSON
17, 23, 40 top, 43 bottom, 48 bottom,
49, 60, 61, 94, 95, 174 top

HILLYER PHOTOGRAPHY INC.,
JONATHON
100, 101
■

IMES, BIRNEY
54, 55
■

JACOBS, JEFFREY/MIM STUDIOS
164 top, 165

JORDAN PHOTOGRAPHY, JENNIFER
186, 187, 210
■

KLEIN & WILSON
74, 75
■

LENTINI, JIM AND STEVE PERRY
224 bottom

LITTLE, CHRIS A.
98, 99

LOTT, HAL
167, 174 bottom, 175, 194, 195
■

MADER, BOB
126 top

MARTIN, SPIDER
38, 39

MCGEE, E. ALAN
214 bottom

MIMS, ALAN/MIM STUDIOS
25, 86 top, 87

MONTGOMERY, IRA
166

MOORE, RIC
161

MORELAND, MIKE
215

MUIR, ROB
40 bottom, 41, 42, 43 top, 48 top, 96,
200, 201

MURPHY, KEN
26 bottom, 27

NICHOLS, MARY E.
97

PERRY, STEVE AND JIM LENTINI
224 bottom

PISANO, ROBERT
92, 93

PORTER, WILLIAM A.
119

PURYEAR PHOTOGRAPHY, JACK
183

RAMSEY, MARY ANN
71

RICHMOND, DAVE
90 top

ROGERS PHOTOGRAPHY, JOHN
78, 79, 210 bottom, 211

ROSE, KEVIN C.
28 bottom

ROTHSCHILD, BILL
132 bottom, 146, 147

SARGENT, KIM/SARGENT AND
ASSOCIATES
9, 142, 143, 164 bottom, 168, 169,
190, 191, 202, 203, 228 top, 229,
230 bottom

SCHILLING, DAVID/SCHILLING
PHOTOGRAPHY
19, 21, 30, 31, 52, 62, 63, 64,
65, 66, 68, 69, 82, 83, 102, 103,
118 top, 122, 123, 124 bottom,
128 bottom, 129, 138, 139, 148,
149, 158, 159, 178, 179, 189 bottom,
208, 209, 212, 213, 218, 219,
220, 221, 228 bottom
'Property of Veranda'

SHIELDS, CURT
160 top

SMALLING, WALTER
50

SNORTUM STUDIO, MARTY
58, 59

STEPHENSON PHOTOGRAPHY,
AARON
226 bottom

SURLOFF, MARK
32, 33

TATA PHOTOGRAPHY, PETER
182 bottom

UGARTE, ANTONIO
156 bottom

VIDAURRE, JOSE MANUEL
136 top, 137

VITALE, PETER
36 bottom, 37, 51, 114 top

VON SCHULENBURG, FRITZ
188, 189 TOP

WAKELY, MICHAEL
196 bottom

WEIGLER, JACK
126 bottom, 127

WILKINS, FREDA
76, 77

WITTMAYER PHOTOGRAPHERS, INC.
105

WRIGHT COMMUNICATIONS
192, 193

WRISLEY, BARD
214 top

YOCHUM, JAMES
110, 111